BUILDING THE SKAGIT

BY PAUL C. PITZER

Pictures courtesy of Seattle City Light, Seattle Municipal Archives and the Whatcom County Museum of History & Art.

City Light thanks Jeff Jewell, Whatcom County Museum of History & Art, and Scott Cline and Anne Frantilla, Seattle Municipal Archives, for their assistance.

"Building the Skagit" was originally published in 1978 by The Galley Press and was reprinted twice. This book is a substanially revised edition.

Seattle City Light
Seattle, Washington 98104

ISBN 0-9712573-0-2

TABLE OF CONTENTS

Introduction 1
A Little Gold, A Lot of Noise 3
Homesteaders and Headaches 11
Let's Build a Dam - Somewhere 21
Let's Build Another Dam - Somewhere Else 37
Step Right This Way, Folks 51
Gold! Again? 59
Ruby to the War 65
The Postwar Boom 69
Back Where We Started 77
Epilogue 81

MAPS

Washington State .... inside front cover
The Skagit River iv
Upper Skagit Mining Areas 8
Hydroelectric Sites 27
The Skagit Dams 83

Diablo Dam construction, August 18, 1930

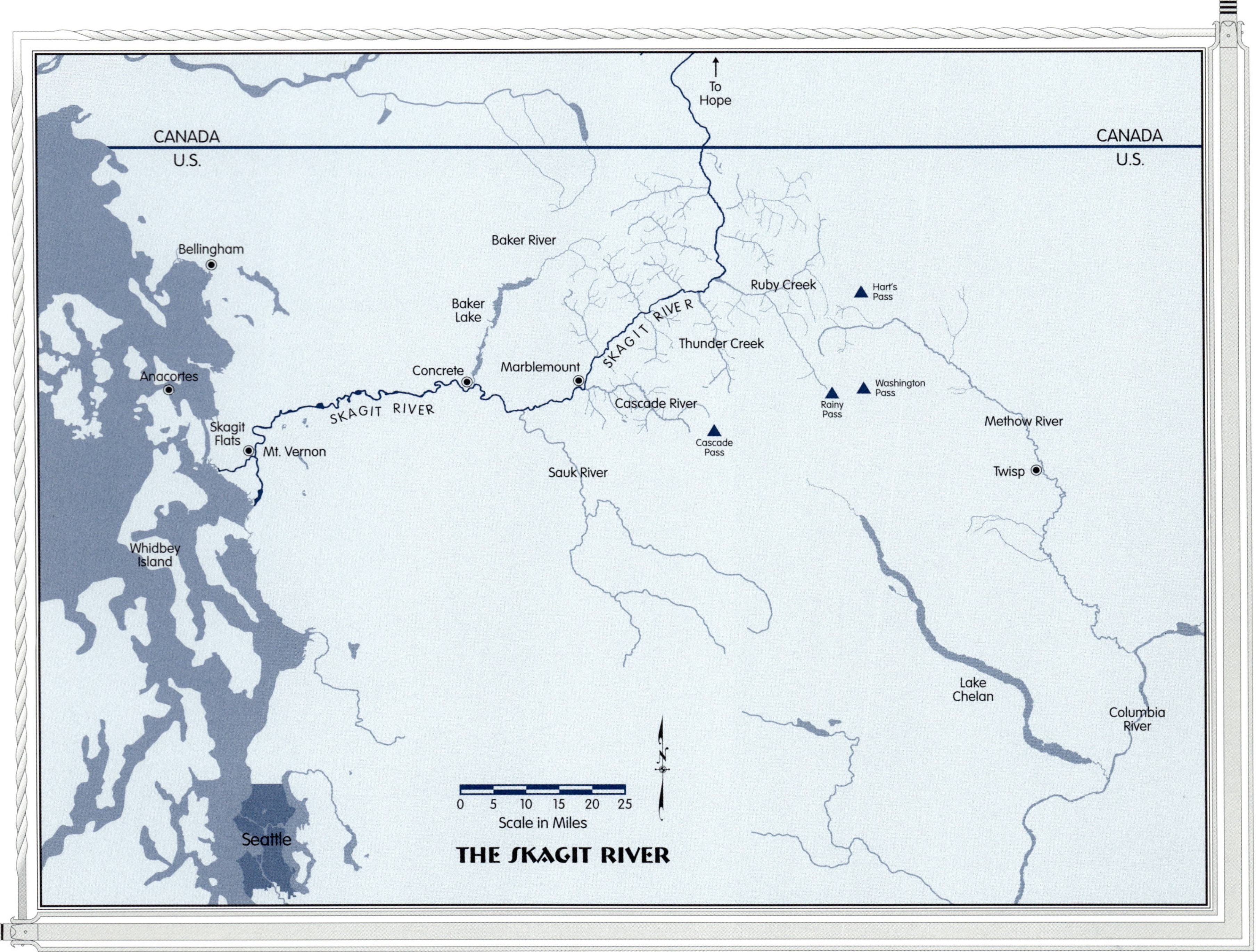
To
Hope
CANADA
U.S.
CANADA
U.S.
Bellingham
Baker River
Baker
Lake
Ruby Creek
Hart's
Pass
SKAGIT RIVER
Thunder Creek
Anacortes
Concrete
Marblemount
Washington
Pass
Rainy
Pass
Cascade River
SKAGIT RIVER
Skagit
Flats
Mt. Vernon
Cascade
Pass
Methow River
Sauk River
Twisp
Whidbey
Island
Lake
Chelan
Columbia
River
0 5 10 15 20 25
Scale in Miles
N
Seattle
THE SKAGIT RIVER

INTRODUCTION

The drive across northern Washington's scenic cross-state highway is a beautiful trip, offering the tourist some of the most spectacular vistas found anywhere. And the drive from Mount Vernon to Twisp can be made so easily today that it is hard to imagine the difficulties faced by the early explorers and developers of the Upper Skagit. But look at the names of the mountains and valleys en route and you will gain a feeling for the colorful history of the area.

Above Concrete are Teebone Ridge, Mount Despair, Mount Fury, Lonesome Creek, Damnation Creek, Phantom Pass, Mount Terror and Bald Eagle Creek. Farther along lie Sky Creek, the Devil's Dome, Nightmare Camp, Desolation Peak, Mount Prophet, Big Devil and Little Devil Mountains, Diablo Canyon, Mount Challenger, Inspiration Peak, Razor Back Mountain, Jackass Mountain, Bald Mountain, Goat Mountain, Ragged Ridge, Easy Peak and Joker Mountain. Those were the names given the features by the miners who worked along the Upper Skagit in the 1880s and they pretty well explain why so little happened in that part of Washington until after gold was discovered there.

In those days the river flowed free, swift and cold; the mountains were rugged and unclimbed and the weather could turn ugly in a hurry. Today, the only feature that remains unchanged is the weather and it closes down the new highway for a few months every winter, just to prove that it is still a force with which to be reckoned. Driving from Marblemount to Ruby Creek takes about 40 minutes now, not two or three days of hard hiking. The old homesteaders would hardly recognize the place and would probably pass it by as being far too civilized. So let's look back at the first 100 years on the Upper Skagit, after the arrival of the white man. The taming of the river and its subsequent development are themselves an interesting tale. But the history of the Skagit mirrors, in microcosm, the history of all public lands in the western United States, the shifting philosophy of the Forest Service and the growth of the environmental and conservation movements that have become so important. From 1870 until 1970, the Upper Skagit was built into a formidable hydroelectric project and a national recreation area. It took a lot of men, a lot of time, an awful lot of money and it produced a story worth telling.

Diablo Dam construction, 1921.

Diablo Dam spilling.

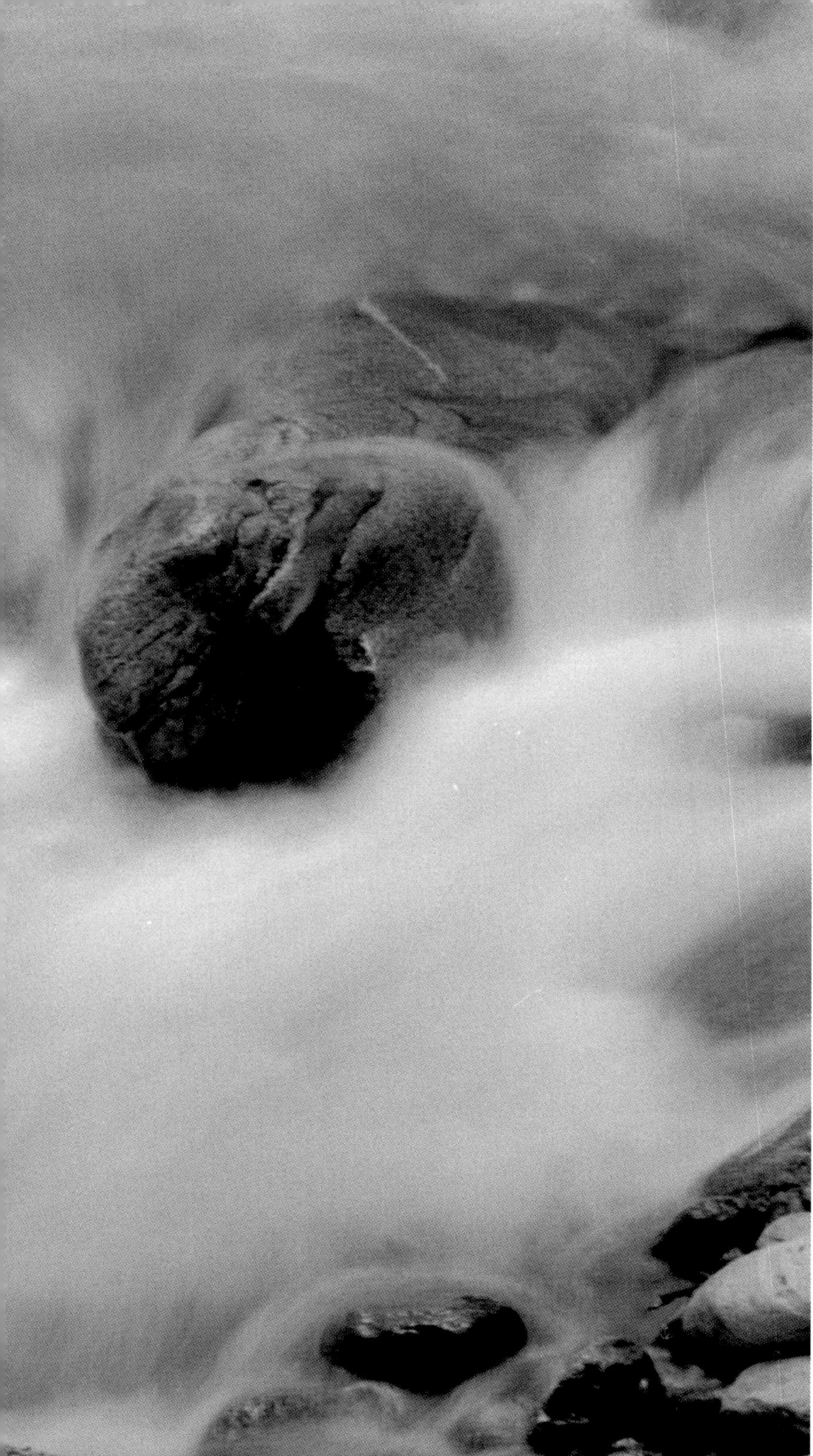

Chapter 1

A Little Gold, A Lot of Noise

Our look at the Skagit starts off with a bit of a mystery. No one knows for sure who discovered the river and this is understandable. Near its mouth, where it enters Puget Sound, the Skagit divides into a collection of sluggish streams and sloughs that wander slowly across what is called the Skagit Flats. From a boat on the Sound it is hard to say for sure that there really is a river there at all, let alone the second largest river in Washington state.

Perhaps the Spanish navigator Lieutenant Francisco Eliza saw parts of the Skagit in 1790 while he was sailing into Bellingham Bay. But we remember him today only because he named Mount Baker, calling it Montana del Carmelo. In 1792, Joseph Whidbey explored Puget Sound, renamed it Mount Baker after a member of his crew and an island after himself. Whidbey even met some of the Indians who lived around the Skagit but he made no record of finding a river.

Alexander Ross, an explorer for the Hudson's Bay Company, trooped through the Upper Skagit Valley in 1824 but it is doubtful that Ross always knew where he was and the Hudson's Bay Company was interested only in furs. So it discouraged prospecting or the intrusion of foreigners into areas it considered exclusively its own. That all ended in 1846 when the boundary between the United States and Canada was finally fixed at the 49th parallel. But the rush for gold in California followed by similar excitement in Eastern Washington at Colville in 1855 and along the Fraser River in 1858 kept sincere miners far away from the Skagit.

A few visitors must have wandered beyond the Skagit Flats during those years but the records are slim and there are indications that once anyone ventured into the narrow valley along the swift river they quickly turned around and headed back downstream. Settlements were growing all along Puget Sound during that time and there was curiosity about what might be found in the hills to the east. But most of the farmers on the flats were too busy trying to make a living to waste time beating their way upriver on an adventure that might prove nothing more than a lot of exercise.

In 1877, a rumor spread that gold had been found in huge quantities (the way gold is always found) beyond the mountains in the Methow Valley. That was serious business, well worth investigating. Six settlers – Otto Klement, Charles von Pressentin, Jack Rowley, Frank Scott, John Duncan and John Sutter – hired two Indian brothers named Charlie and Joe Seaam as guides, jumped into their canoes and started off toward the Okanogan country. They followed the Skagit up to what is today called the Cascade River, then continued on until they arrived at Lake Chelan, where they found no gold, then returned home.

They figured the summer was already interrupted so they regrouped and returned to the Upper Skagit, up to Ruby Creek, where they found traces of gold here and there but were driven back downriver by bad weather.[1] The eight men returned next summer and found more gold; not much, but enough to make a good story when they were back home.

In 1879, Albert Bacon, another Skagit Flats farmer, led a group of friends upriver and staked out the Nip and Tuck mine eight miles above Ruby Creek, the first mine on the river. At the same time, Jack Rowley was leading a second group up the Skagit. As they camped by a creek one night, Rowley had a dream in which he saw a great "hidden hand" pointing the way to Canyon Creek and indicating that gold would be found there. Sure enough, Rowley staked out the Discovery Mine and was $1,000 richer by the end of the summer. Bacon did even better, taking more than $1,500 worth of gold out of the Nip and Tuck.

Bacon later sold his mine to a black prospector named George Holmes who took $7,000 worth of gold out over a period of years and lived on the site until 1924. He then left the valley and was never heard of again.[2]

Needless to say, when Rowley and Bacon returned to Skagit Flats, word of their find touched off a gold rush. The years 1879 and 1880 saw the first of many migrations up the Skagit, with men in search of instant, easy wealth. What a disappointment the cold, rainy, inhospitable place must have been to most of them. They traveled along the river as far as possible on steamers from Seattle. Then they switched to canoes and finally finished the trip on foot. "Great Excitement Prevails at La Conner" headlined the Bellingham Bay Mail in July 1880.[3] One of the miners reported, "Ruby Creek is said to have gold from one end to the other..."[4] Actually, the miners averaged about a $1.50 worth of gold a day, but that was because they were only just reaching the layers where the real gold was located, they said.

Someone proposed that a company be formed to make huge hot-air balloons that could carry men to the mines and eliminate the dangerous trip upriver. Indeed, during the peak of the rush it was not uncommon to see bodies floating past Mount Vernon and it was obvious that there were many luckless men who never made it to the gold fields. The trail was narrow, nonexistent in places, and when the weather was bad, which was most of the time, there were more hazards than gold.

Into the picture stepped a man named N. E. Goodell, after whom Goodell Creek, near present-day Newhalem, is named. Goodell packed $1,000 worth of supplies up the Skagit to a site near the creek that bears his name. He sold the goods to miners at a loss, however, because no one had any money and returned in the fall poorer, but still excited about the riches that would be found eventually. Goodell toured Seattle, made speeches saying that the rush to the Skagit would bring money into Seattle; that the merchants of Victoria, B.C., would snatch the opportunity away if Seattle was not careful. He raised more than $2,000 which was earmarked for construction of the Ruby Creek Trail.[5]

Building a trail or road up the Skagit is a thread that runs through its history. The job was not completed until almost 100 years after Goodell made his first proposals and collected his money.

Gold or no gold, the miners came. Some managed to guide their boats up the Skagit as far as a place called The Portage, about seven miles below Goodell Creek. From there they walked. Many went to Canada, then along the Fraser River to Fort Hope and south to the Skagit. They had to leave their provisions in bond during the trip through Canada, to avoid paying duty on some items, but the inconvenience seemed worth it, especially when compared with the problems of the other route to the mines.

Above Goodell's camp was a spot where miners had to climb a Jacob's Ladder, up a 40-foot cliff. The trail, such as it was, crossed the river three times in the few miles above Goodell's. In winter there was heavy snow, high water and avalanches, not to mention wind and biting cold. If there were no snow slides, there were rock and mud slides. The miners could take their choice.

This all would be set straight, however, with Goodell's collected money and by the company that gave him the lowest bid for building the trail. But when the trail crew arrived, it took one look and offered to pay off the contract, wanting only to leave and forget the whole thing. Some work was done on the trail later by various mining companies but it was haphazard and minimal.

In May 1880, the first big mining company was organized and, oddly enough, it was formed in Portland, Ore. It was an ambitious group and it planned to locate, purchase, hold, develop, sell and transfer mining claims, locate water rights, import hydraulic machinery, build ditches and erect mills. With such a bold company on the scene, the success of the Ruby Mines was guaranteed, everyone thought. Ruby City, a tent town near the mines, was growing and some miners were realizing up to $8 worth of gold a day. But the Skagit Mining Company went broke after 30 days and out of existence.[6]

The miners worked hard around Ruby Creek and removed the little bit of placer gold that was there. But it was hardly enough to make anybody rich and the big rush was over by the fall of 1880. Nearly everyone, including Goodell, packed up and left.

Some say that 5,000 miners or more joined that first gold rush on the Skagit but that is an exaggeration. A census report made at the high point of the activity produced only 519 names. Assuming that some of the miners were off prospecting when the survey was taken, that would still put 1,000 as a high figure, 1,500 at the outside. Although the first rush was unproductive, the Upper Skagit had at last been explored and some richly descriptive names had been attached to its features. The rush also proved that if any more gold was there, it would be mined the hard way. It required the efforts of large companies with adequate capital investment who could afford to build a good trail up the narrow valley, import stamp mills and other heavy machinery.

In the decade following the 1880 rush there was some activity on the Upper Skagit. Early in the 1890s, a few small companies sent crews up to both Ruby and Thunder creeks where they found small amounts of gold-bearing quartz ore and sent it down the valley to be refined. But there was no profit in that. One colorful prospector named Jack Durand formed the Colonial Company and worked at his diggings around Thunder Creek. The mine went broke and Durand is remembered today for two buildings he erected. The first, 13 miles from the mouth of Thunder Creek, is called Middle Cabin and it still serves as a mile post and shelter for hikers. The second, in Marblemount, is called the Log House Inn.

Goodell Creek sawmill, 1920

In 1894, another flurry of activity brought men to the Upper Skagit. It began three years earlier when Alec Barron of Anacortes started working his mine at Slate Creek, just west of Hart's Pass.[7] He found an unusually large amount of gold and this rekindled interest in the Skagit mines. More miners headed for the area again. In 1893 a 400-pound block of high-grade gold ore was taken from the Barron Mines and carted down the still-primitive trail to the coast. From there it was shipped to Chicago and exhibited at the World's Fair.[8]

With reports circulating that Barron was finding up to $12,000 worth of gold each week, more were again excited about the Upper Skagit. A town named Barron was built near the mine, a trail ran from Barron into the Okanogan country through Hart's Pass and some improvements were made on the Skagit trail. Because of the difficult passage up the Skagit, most of the activity at Barron centered on building a road in from the east and parts of a narrow-gauge wagon road were finished by the late 1890s.[9]

By 1900 there were perhaps a half dozen large stamp mills operating near Barron and there were many companies mining, and eventually going broke. Some still exist today, on paper anyway, and they include familiar Upper Skagit names such as Azurite, Gold Hill, Bonita, Mammoth, Chancellor, Anacortes and, of course, Barron.

But the end was in sight in 1897 when news of the Klondike gold rush came. Most miners began moving north and only a few remained to work the meager diggings. Ironically, when the road over Hart's Pass was completed in 1903, the town of Barron was nearly deserted.[10]

There had been many financial disasters. The Ruby Creek Mining Company spent more than $300,000 building its camp, sawmill, bunkhouse and cookhouse on the gravel bar that formed where Ruby Creek ran into the Skagit. The heavy nozzle for its hydraulic operation was mounted on a block of cast iron, packed in by horses. And after all that money and effort, the company managed to scrape only $3,000 worth of gold out of the gravel. It abandoned the holdings and sold the site to a roadhouse operator who called it

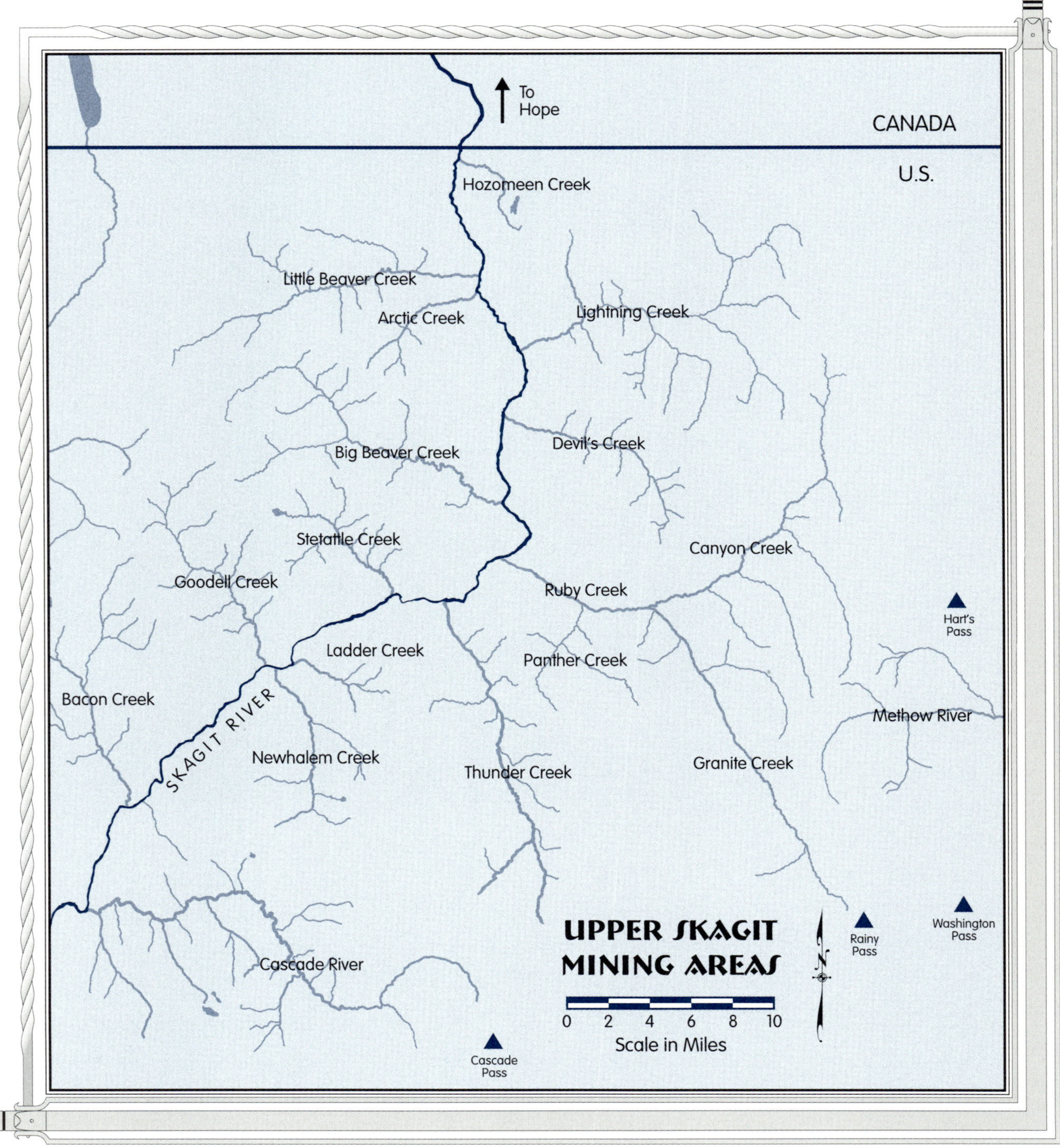

the Ruby Creek Inn. It stood until it was flooded by Ross Lake, nearly 50 years later.

Between 1900 and 1906 the Good-Enough Fraction, the Hub, the Daisy, the Fidelity Extension, the Kent, the Virtue Extension, the Evergreen and the War Eagle companies worked their claims and went broke. The companies with more money carted in their stamp mills and, aided by that degree of mechanization, the Eureka, Mammoth and North American mines outlasted their competitors, but only for a while.

In 1906, an event foreshadowed the eventual development of the river and showed where the real wealth of the Skagit was to be found. A group carried a water wheel through Hart's Pass to Ruby Creek and installed it. They turned it with water diverted over a 2,000-foot flume and hooked it to a generator that supplied electricity to the settlements at the Hyde, Mazama, Azurite and Chancellor mines. The Chancellor was the largest, with a capital stock investment of $200,000. Of course they all went broke and the power plant stopped working. Then the Chancellor Company's engineer, a man named Nicolai Aall, left to join a group that was forming the Skagit Power Company, which we will hear more about later.

After 1900, as far as gold goes, the picture at Ruby Creek is one of decline. Emphasis shifted west to Thunder Creek where no one ever found much gold. But they did find silver. The Mount Vernon Argus was bold enough to predict in 1908 that the new Leadville had been discovered, with 20 rich veins of ore exposed and more just waiting to make men wealthy.[11]

Mining silver is expensive and the companies that promised certain riches at Thunder Creek needed more money from their stockholders. The North Coast Mining and Milling Company incorporated in Tacoma with a stock issue of $1.6 million. The company said the ore on its claim was worth $40 a ton, though they pointed out in the fine print that even $10 a ton would realize a profit. The company would return $2,000 a day to stockholders, it said. In fact, the rich veins of ore pinched out just below the surface and the miners were lucky to realize $4 a ton for their labors. By 1919 the company was gone.

Other companies kept regrouping, renaming themselves and seeking gold or silver with new stockholders behind them. There was the Silver Tip Company, which refinanced as the Standard Reduction and Development Company and later merged with a few others to avoid the inevitable bankruptcy. In most cases, the energy spent on corporate and financial manipulation far exceeded anything that was invested in actual mining.

It would be unfair not to acknowledge the Skagit Queen Mining Company. It was the biggest operator on Thunder Creek or, actually, on Skagit Queen Creek, a tributary of Thunder Creek. The company started in 1905, incorporated for more than $1 million. During the next few years the company built bunkhouses, cookhouses, store houses, powder houses, barns and even a laboratory at its claim site. The claims encompassed 29 separate lodes, it said. This achievement was notable when one remembers that the company still had to haul all its equipment in over the still largely unimproved trail. The company even brought in a water wheel and a generator to furnish power for drilling at the various mines and was ambitious enough to lay out more than a dozen sites for major development. They boldly proclaimed that the ore came from veins of "unending richness." The Skagit Queen even absorbed some of its neighbors and changed its name to the Skagit Queen Consolidated Mining Company.[12] It doubled its capital stock, grew and dug tunnels more than 100 feet long into the mountains.

But it was the same old story. A few feet below the surface, what silver there was gave out and the best the Skagit Queen could manage was $3 to $4 a ton for its ore. The North Cascades granite is hard and unyielding. The Skagit Queen went under still trying and, in 1913, the remaining assets of the company were sold to a group called the British Mining Company. The group, in turn, had evolved from a misguided outfit named the Puget Sound, Chelan and Spokane Railway Company. It invested more money in the old sites, built a new power station, dug a 600-foot foot shaft into the mountain where they expected to tap a rich vein of silver, but found very little for their troubles.

There were a few more mining efforts through the mid-1920s, but nothing of note. The failure of the Thunder Creek mines was as complete as the failure at Ruby Creek 30 years earlier. From 1915 through the mid-1930s, there was only limited prospecting or mining activity on the Skagit. Our focus must shift from the mines to another group who moved up the Skagit – the homesteaders.

Chapter 2

Homesteaders and Headaches

There may be good farming on the Skagit Flats but upstream, especially east of the Baker River, the spots wide enough to move a plow are few. The first settlers in the upper valley came more to sell goods to the miners and to operate roadhouses than to till the soil. For a while they set up housekeeping wherever they could find enough space, clear the trees and raise a shelter from the ever-present rain. But in 1898 the Upper Skagit was included in the Washington Forest Reserve and, in 1906, the Forest Homestead Act stopped further random settlement. This also presented problems for the settlers already there. Just getting there itself still was no easy task, considering the condition of the trail.

The Skagit Trail, called the Goat Trail by most of those who used it, began at Goodell's Landing and followed the river past what is today called Newhalem Creek, past Ladder Creek and up to the Devil's Corner. The Corner is rock outcropping that forced the trail across the river. A few bridges were built there but they either were washed away by floods

Devil's Corner, Skagit River below Gorge Creek. Seattle Municipal Archives

or were destroyed by fires that came during the rare dry summers.

In time there was a trail of sorts around the Devil's Corner. An old hermit called Captain Randolf built a shed for himself perched among the rocks and he chiseled a crude foot path in the rock. Then he collected a toll from everyone who used it. The miners later dynamited a horse trail into the cliff and added handrails. But the Devil's Corner still was the most dangerous spot on the Skagit. The cut in the rock is bypassed today but it still can be seen if a few seconds are spent looking over the edge of the road just above the tunnel nearest the Gorge Powerhouse.

Beyond the Devil's Corner was Hanging Rock Camp. A large rock had fallen and landed in such a way that there was a hollow under it that provided some shelter. It was a good place to rest because the next 40 feet or so were straight up the Jacob's Ladder that had served as the trail since the 1880 gold rush.

The trail crossed Gorge Creek, wound past Midway Creek (called Ketchum Creek today) and up to Cedar Bar, which was just below Tunnel Bar. It was later named Box Canyon, then Diablo Canyon and Diablo Dam is there today.

For a few years there was a bridge across the river at Cedar Bar. But one summer the area was infested by hornets and when an angry miner tried to burn them out he also eliminated the bridge and most of the surrounding forest. Beyond Cedar Bar, the trail ran alongside Stetattle Mountain (now called Davis Mountain), up Sourdough Mountain, past Box Canyon and down into the Punch Bowl, a hollow east of the narrow canyon that is now flooded by Diablo Lake. Then there were six more miles up to Ruby Creek and perhaps twice that distance to the mines, depending on which one you wanted. It was about a three-day hike, depending on the weather. Think about that when you drive through there today at 55 miles an hour.

Negotiating the trail was a daily task for the people who lived along the Skagit. These homesteaders came and went as they

Photo courtesy of Whatcom County Museum of History & Art

pleased until 1906 when the Forest Homestead Act ruled that they could keep their claims only if they had lived on them for five years prior to the passage of the act. No claim could be larger than 160 acres and no valuable timber land could be included. All claims had to be primarily agricultural. If the settler could convince Forest Service officials that his claim was legitimate, the land was surveyed and became private property.[1]

Among the first of the Skagit residents to apply was a spunky little woman named Lucinda Davis. She was the daughter of a Methodist minister in Pennsylvania, had divorced her husband in Colorado in 1890 and moved with her three young children to the home of her brother, George Leach. Leach had lived along the Cascade River and had drowned there a few months earlier. Lucinda and the children farmed in the summers and moved to Mount Vernon in the winters to be near a school. Seven years later, the Cascade River flooded and washed away the Davis farmhouse. Undaunted, Lucinda looked upstream and decided to move to Cedar Bar, along the route to the mines. There was an old cabin where some Indians had lived and the Davis family planned to build a roadhouse where miners could stay the night and buy provisions.

Each spring the four Davises opened their roadhouse around mid-April, depending on the weather. They also raised hay and sold it to travelers for their horses. Glee Davis, the youngest son, built a water wheel on Stetattle Creek, added a grist mill and ground flour. About 1900, a flood carried away the mill and a fire burned the roadhouse to the ground. It was a bad year.

They rebuilt the roadhouse in time for the next summer's traffic and carried on. In 1906, they filed for their claim under the new Homestead Act. When the ranger arrived to look the place over, he argued with Lucinda Davis about his board and room bill, disagreed about where the claim boundaries should be and decided that the Davis family was out to get a monopoly on business in that part of the valley. So he wrote a negative report, suggesting the Davis homestead be used as a ranger station site and that the Davis family be sent packing.[2]

The Davis family had actually asked for considerably more than the 160 acres allowed, but the ranger had suggested they should have no more than 43 acres, if they got any at all. Lucinda Davis reduced her request to the maximum 160 acres, refiled and two years later was still waiting for an answer.

The Forest Service philosophy, at that time, held that the public lands should be used in a way that would benefit the largest number of people. It felt that homesteaders were only a nuisance in the way of progress. The Forest Service reports on the Davis ranch noted that if there was ever any logging in the Upper Skagit Valley, the location of the Davis ranch would prohibit construction of a railroad necessary to remove the timber. So the Forest Service wrote Lucinda Davis a letter telling her she might or might not win her claim, but if she did a right-of-way would be established on the property so that a trail or railroad could be built at some future date.

Lucinda Davis was irked by the delay and wrote directly to Forest Service Director Gifford Pinchot. She explained that a claim of 43 acres would remove from her control the little bit of timber she had on the land and that the Forest Service should be thankful that she took care of the place, quelling fires in the summer and doing other maintenance work.

Davis Ranch, 2 1/2 miles above the Gorge Dam site, Skagit River. Seattle Municipal Archives

The Forest Service replied that the Davis family might be granted a special-use permit, enabling them to run their roadhouse in the event their claim was ultimately refused. The letter pointed out that other good citizens also fought fires and did not require special thanks or payment.

The Davis family gave up the next spring, filed a claim for the 43 acres that had been more or less approved and waited. The claim was about ready for final action four years later, in 1912, but then Congress ordered a survey of all federal forest lands. That delayed resolution for another two years. Glee Davis got into an argument with the forest rangers about the location of trails through and around the Davis homestead and that caused more delays. Lucinda Davis was finally awarded her claim on June 15, 1917, 11 years after she had filed.

In 1913, Glee Davis married and his wife, Hazel, moved to the homestead. The other Davis children had long since married and moved away. Glee ran the roadhouse and worked for, of all organizations, the Forest Service, building trails and lookout stations. Glee's brother, Frank, later moved back to Cedar Bar and they built a dam across Stetattle Creek, constructed a 2,000- foot flume that ran to the homestead and carried water to irrigate their garden. Years later, in 1925, Glee and his brother acquired a quarter-horse generator, which they installed on Cedar Bar. But they only enjoyed the luxury of electricity for a while because Seattle City Light was building in the valley and had acquired most of the land around the Davis homestead. After two long court battles over condemnation proceedings, City Light paid the Davis family about $26,000 and took over the holdings at Cedar Bar. In 1929, Lucinda Davis, by then an old woman, and her family moved down the valley. Less than a year later, Lucinda Davis was dead.

We must consider the possibility that the Forest Service was right and that the Davis family should have been denied the homestead claim. But the evidence shows that the real debate was over just who would use the public land and benefit from it. Obviously the settlers were looking out for their own interests and the Forest Service supported large-scale development by big companies or even public agencies. The homesteaders had a legal right to own their land but the law and the presumptions of the Forest Service were at odds, and August Dohne's story well illustrates what happened.

When gold rush promoter Goodell packed up and left the Upper Skagit, he sold his place on Goodell Creek to Henry Dennis, who sold it a few years later to August Dohne. Dohne was born in Germany in 1851 and had migrated to the Dakotas where he lived for a while. In 1893 he moved to a claim downriver from Goodell's Landing but left it in 1897 when he bought the buildings at Goodell Creek from Dennis. Dohne worked hard to improve the place and the final touch was a large, two-story, cedar cabin with eight rooms, a bunkhouse, a barn and a few other smaller buildings.[3]

Dohne had plowed three acres and had cleared 10 more. There was an estimated 6 million board feet of timber on the 124 acres he claimed, clearly more than the law allowed. Nevertheless, Dohne filed for his land and a forest ranger inspected it a few weeks later. Judging by his report, the ranger was impressed and he called Dohne "a credit to the community."[4] The report recommended that Dohne be awarded his land and no mention was made of the timber.

But it was not that easy. About that time a new superintendent, Charles Park, was sent to manage the forest reserve and Park rejected private ownership whenever possible. He also was involved in some business dealings himself and was interested in the men who were starting the Skagit Power Co. So was ranger Alfred B. Conrad, stationed in Rockport. Conrad, upset about Dohne's claim, sent a letter to Park which said in part, "Dohne is trying to claim land needed by the 'Power Company' and this company would rather deal with the government. Look into it!"[5]

The two rangers speculated that Dohne had laid out his claim to purposely include the land needed by the power company and that he had no right to that land. In talks with representatives of the Skagit Power Co., Park was told that Dohne's claim would delay progress indefinitely and the power company urged that some, if not all, of the claim be denied.[6]

They needed a way to discredit Dohne, or some legal grounds on which to challenge his claim. The first tack was to prove that the boundaries had been altered. But surveys and talks with the neighbors indicated that Dohne had been scrupulously honest.

The forest rangers next pointed out that a ranger station site had been established on part of the Dohne claim prior to any action by the old German settler, but Dohne produced mining and deed notices that he had recorded as early as 1898, ending that maneuver.

Early in 1909, Park and Conrad found William Thornton, an old neighbor of Dohne's who had known the German before he moved to Goodell Creek. Dohne and Thornton never got along and Thornton happily described his old adversary as, "not quite responsible, sometimes."[7] That was all Park needed and he planned to take Dohne to court, charging that the claim boundaries were not the originals drawn by either Goodell or Henry Dennis and that he had a witness who knew Dohne to be less than honest. Gloating, Park wrote to Conrad that he would, "..... use Thornton for all he's worth."[8]

Panning for gold in the Upper Skagit River Valley.

But the plan fell apart when Henry Dennis appeared and verified the boundaries of Dohne's claim. Park was furious and, still determined to undo the Dohne claim, dug deeper into the records, even writing to Washington, D.C., for information. He found what he wanted late in 1909. Dohne had filed a claim on some government land in 1885 in North Dakota and the law said no one could have more than one claim. Park's happiness was short-lived when Dohne produced evidence that he had relinquished the North Dakota claim and was thus entitled to his Upper Skagit land.

Park then challenged Dohne on the grounds that he was not a citizen but Dohne produced his naturalization papers and, furthermore, Park was informed that citizenship was not required to homestead. Unable to delay it any longer, Park and Conrad held a preliminary hearing on Dohne's claim in December 1909. All the evidence indicated it was legitimate but Park ruled the findings were inconclusive and postponed a decision so that more evidence could be found.

Early in 1910, the Skagit Power Co. decided not to build on the Skagit, preferring another site it had found on the Cascade River. Three months later, Dohne's claim was granted and he was given title to his land. In the rush to complete the proceedings, the Forest Service again overlooked the timber Dohne had acquired in the deal.

Dohne's roadhouse burned to the ground in 1913 and was rebuilt a year later it. In 1918, the old homesteader took sick, moved to a hospital down the valley and died. His land was sold by the probate court, ending up in the hands of a Sedro Woolley investment company. It sold the claim to Seattle City Light a few months later.

The Davis family and Dohne had problems claiming their land because the Forest Service saw them as a threat to developers who were planning to build along the Upper Skagit.

The stories are more striking when we consider the case of John McMillan. McMillan was born in Ontario in 1854 and settled on the Skagit in 1884. He had a homestead near Big Beaver Creek, north of Ruby Creek and far from the centers of development. Oddly enough, he never applied for his land, yet Forest Service officials left him alone, though they knew that he was there.

McMillan had an Indian wife and they, with some of her friends, lived in a shack on their claim until 1900. Then McMillan traveled to Seattle, stayed longer than expected and, in the process, married a woman named Emma Love. After their honeymoon, McMillan and his new wife moved up to Big Beaver Creek and McMillan drove away the Indian woman and her friends. McMillan and his new wife farmed a little, sold supplies to miners and lived happily on the land until 1922 when he died. His widow returned to Seattle and the land was abandoned. Never was there a formal claim made and not once did the Forest Service bother the isolated couple. But no one else wanted the land either and it was clearly of no use to the developers. That made all the difference.

Hotel Cedar Bar, Darius Kinsey, 1900

Then there was Tommy Rowland. He settled near Big Beaver Creek around 1895 and lived alone there for years. Rowland supported himself by raising vegetables, which he sold to the miners. He was a strange mystic who had visions and who believed he was the reincarnation of the prophet Elisha. In one of his more spiritual moments, he dubbed his shack and land The New Jerusalem. Because of his peculiarities, he was a constant subject of conversation among the miners and a rumor started that crazy old Tommy had found a lot of gold around his place and he really was about as crazy as a fox. A group of the miners talked Tommy Rowland into traveling down the valley with them and while they were in Sedro Woolley they had him committed to the mental hospital.

When they returned, the miners checked Rowland's cabin and found, to their disappointment, that he was as poor as a church mouse and maybe more so. Meanwhile, Rowland took exception to living in the asylum and managed to escape. He made his way back to his New Jerusalem, where he avoided harm's way for a few years but a couple of Forest Service rangers finally caught him. As they took him back down the valley he had one last look at his beloved home from a high point along the trail. With a biblical presence, Rowland waved his hands and announced that if he could not live in the New Jerusalem he wished it destroyed so that nobody could live there ever again. He was returned to the hospital, where he died after a few months. Tommy Rowland never saw New Jerusalem again. Since 1949, no one else has seen it either because it is now under Ross Lake.

Another homesteader who lost his land was Burton Babcock. Babcock was born in Iowa in 1858 and he moved west in the 1880s, settling on a piece of land just below Goodell Creek. From

1892 through 1897 he usually was somewhere in the valley, prospecting or working as a hired hand. The second gold rush on Ruby Creek had ended and when Klondike fever hit the Upper Skagit, Babcock suffered a particularly bad case.

In Iowa, Babcock had grown up with Hamlin Garland, who later became a famous writer. Garland was always on the lookout for experiences around which he could weave his stories and he too was touched by the mystique of the Yukon. The two friends corresponded over the years and when Babcock expressed interest in going north, Garland offered to hire his old friend as a guide and odd-job man, while he paid the bills and recorded the trip in his diary. The adventure was as wonderful as Garland had hoped and he recounted the adventure in two of his books: "Trail of the Goldseekers" and "Daughter of the Middle Border."

When he was full of happy experiences, Garland returned home, leaving Babcock to wander a while longer seeking gold. In 1904, Babcock returned to his Skagit claim, not a penny richer than the day he left. All would have been well except that the Yukon trip meant Babcock had not resided on his land five continuous years prior to 1906. Carefully avoiding officials, the wily Babcock waited until after 1908 to file his land claim but the officials pointed out the residency problem and rejected it.[9]

Babcock contacted his old friend, Hamlin Garland. Garland, in turn, wrote a letter to Chief Forester Gifford Pinchot, whom he had met through a mutual friend, Theodore Roosevelt. One would assume that, with such friends in high places pulling strings, Babcock would have been given his land, but he wasn't. Pinchot answered that Babcock would have to leave the claim.

Garland tried again, writing a second letter to Pinchot recounting the plight of his tired companion: "He is forced to go off the claim to cook for a living, or to cut or dig for somebody else. He hasnt (*sic*) a dollar except what he pounds out of the ends of his fingers and he has worked 10 years of his life on that accursid (*sic*) claim. Why can't you do something for him? I wish you would."[10]

A secretary answered Garland's second letter, saying Babcock might be given a special permit to use the land for a while but that ownership was out of the question. The law was the law and it could not be stretched.

Babcock was stubborn and insisted on owning his land outright. So he wrote a third letter to Garland, adding details to strengthen his case. Armed with new evidence, Garland wrote Pinchot again and his letter bears repeating:

Dear Mr. Pinchot: Mr. Babcock has just written me giving fuller information on his case. It seems he has lived ten years on this land. Five years before going with me to the Klondike and five years since. Of course, he could not live on it continuously for he is a bachelor and very poor. He was obliged to go away to earn money to live on – but he had built on the claim and had been holding it five years when I hired him to go with me to the Northwest. His leaving the claim so long was a mistake but the whole country as I understand it was unsurveyed and no filing possible. Since then he has lived on the claim five years more. It seems to me wanton cruelty to take so much out of a man's life and give nothing in return. I may still be lacking in information for he is not a fluent correspondent but his case seems more and more pitiful as I contemplate it. I hope he can be given the use of the claim with the rights – under your direction – to cut and sell timber. He is one of the most singular men I ever knew – absolutely sober, clean hearted and a thinker. He was at one time a Unitarian preacher but a curious shyness, a kind of stage-fright made speaking so painful that he gave it up. He is as simple as a child in some ways but a lion in courage. He comes of a good strain of New England blood but living alone so much has increased his 'queerness'. He is a shy mystic, wordless when most deeply moved, and to think of him packing salmon with Siwashes or cooking for a gang of railway heads gives me pain. If he can be assured of his claims in some way and permitted to harvest it – under careful direction – he would be saved much mental as well as physical misery. If executive action can help I would like President Roosevelt to read this letter.[11]

But it was impossible. The Forest Service doubted that even the president could help much and when the hearing on Babcock's claim was held in 1909, the claim was denied. Adamant that he be given his land, Babcock rejected a special-use permit and appealed the decision. There were two appeals and Babcock lost both. He was given 90 days to leave the claim.

Babcock moved upstream to Reflector Bar near Diablo Canyon. He found work as a watchman at a Skagit Power Co. exploration site. But he was released after a few months, wandered the valley for a few days, became sick and was taken to Seattle where he stayed with his sister until he died a few weeks later.

It was obvious that the homesteaders, for one reason or another, were not going to develop the Upper Skagit any more than the miners had. The Forest Service vision had triumphed and all that remained was to determine which enterprise would finally succeed in developing the resources of the Skagit.

The companies investigating hydroelectric power already were on the scene.

Chapter 3

Let's Build a Dam – Somewhere

It was obvious to the farmers on the Skagit Flats that dams would have to be built on the Upper Skagit someday. The river flooded almost every year and only a series of barricades across the river could end the annual inundations. If electrical power could be generated at the dams, so much the better. And the lakes behind the dams would provide wonderful recreation areas that many could enjoy. Three birds could be killed with one stone and everyone would benefit. But there was one hitch. Dams then, as now, were expensive and the cost would be recovered only if the power generated could be successfully marketed. It was 90 miles to Seattle as the crow flew and almost as far to Bellingham. And as everyone knew at the turn of the century, transmitting electrical energy that far was out of the question. Large-scale hydroelectric technology was in its infancy and even if money was no problem, building any project on the Skagit would be difficult.

Pony Bridge over Skagit River, Darius Kinsey, 1900. Seattle Municipal Archives

In spite of any risks, if there is money to be made, there are usually people who will try to make it. We have already seen that on a small scale; the mining companies that were using the water power of Skagit tributaries. The Chancellor Mining Co. on Ruby Creek and the Skagit Queen Co. on Thunder Creek each had extensive power developments serving their own and neighboring mines.

An Anacortes man named Charles Freeman probably deserves credit as the first visionary to promote hydroelectric development on the Skagit in a big way. Around 1903 and 1904, he hiked the valley, inspecting the power installations at the mines and envisioning huge projects that might be placed on the main river.[1] Like so many men with ideas, however, Freeman had no money so he needed backers.

Freeman ran into E.M. Biggs, J.S. McCrystal, and M.W. Patrick, representatives of a Denver-based company that was seeking investment possibilities. They were skeptical at first, but finally agreed to at least see the Skagit. In June 1905 the four men crossed the Cascades from the Okanogan country and arrived at Cedar Bar where they stayed at the Davis ranch. They saw the potential and returned to Denver where they invested $1 million and formed the Skagit Power Co. They intended to build a dam on the Skagit, probably at Box Canyon. When they had their tentative ideas on the drawing board, they sent their representative to post notices along the Skagit which stated their intentions. There would be one dam about three miles upriver from August Dohne's claim and another at Box Canyon. Biggs had renamed it Diablo Canyon after a landmark in the Southwest that he said it

The Goat Trail, Skagit River, Darius Kinsey, 1900.
Seattle Municipal Archives

resembled, in a wetter sort of way. Claims were filed with the proper county and state authorities. As it turned out, the witness for the power company, the man who swore that they had proceeded legally and had really put up their signs, was August Dohne.

In 1908 the Skagit Power Co. expanded its plans and proposed dams at four sites. There were the first two, at Goodell's and at Diablo, a third at Ruby Creek and a fourth called the Davis dam site below Cedar Bar. For good measure, it added a fifth location called Hanging Rock, at the confluence of Gorge Creek and the Skagit. After all, it only cost 50 cents to record each claim in Bellingham.

At that time, the rules of the game said that as long as no one actually had a permit to build a specific power project, there was nothing to stop anyone from filing notices saying they intended to build any number of them. The Colorado investors knew that and also knew they were not the only ones interested in the Skagit. They returned to the river, staking out locations for their powerhouses and talking as if it was just a matter of time until they started digging. They envisioned an extensive project costing an unheard-of $6 million that would tame the wild Skagit and generate more power than that part of Washington state could use for a long time to come. The dam at Diablo Canyon alone would be 170 feet high with a power tunnel stretching seven miles through the mountains, ending at the powerhouse above Goodell Creek. There were some less-ambitious alternatives if the project proved too big, but one fact was certain: The Skagit Power Co. was there to stay and, to show good faith, it hired a crew and started to build a road.

The crew began work at Goodell's Landing and worked its way up the narrow valley. After much digging, blasting and considerable cursing, they found that cutting a road through that hard rock was not easy. With a half mile of road bed completed, they quit.

Freeman began to suspect that his friends in the Skagit Power Co. were losing heart for the project. Cost estimates soared out of sight and the investors retreated to Colorado to reconsider. Meanwhile, Freeman trekked the valley, posting and reposting water-rights notices, hoping to scare off others while his own company regrouped.

Freeman's worst fears were realized when he found the postings of would-be competitors. A small outfit in Bellingham, represented by Otto E. Johnson, posted notices around Thunder Creek and

William McAllister of the North Coast Mining and Milling Co. posted them up and down the valley.

It was not unknown for unsuccessful mining companies to change direction and a move into the power business seemed so easy that Freeman must have blanched white when he saw their signs. Then came the Thunder Creek Transportation and Smelting Co. At first its primary interest seemed to be Thunder Creek, but that was too close for Freeman's comfort. When the company posted a few signs around Diablo Canyon and another at the Rip Raps, below Ruby Creek, Freeman was livid.

What Freeman did not know was something his friends in Denver were slowly learning. A large Boston-based holding company, Stone and Webster, had become interested in the Skagit. Wealthy and powerful, Stone and Webster was quietly discouraging investors who were being approached by Skagit Power Co. That explained the inability of the Colorado men to secure financing, but they refused to give up.

In 1910, Skagit Power announced that building anything on the Skagit was too costly and that it would first develop a site it had claimed on the Cascade River. Once in operation, the money earned there would finance the more-expensive Skagit plants. Estimates for a Skagit dam were then up to $8 million and rising. But the Coloradans was adamant that the Cascade dam was only a step toward the company's ultimate goal, building the Skagit dams. They would not relinquish their claims.

Further investigation, however, showed that Skagit Power could not afford to build on the Cascade either. Freeman continued to hike both the Skagit and Cascade rivers, posting notices and trying to keep his dream alive. While he was off on one of his trips,

Skagit River at Ripraps

Biggs sold the company to Stone and Webster for $250,000.[2] The company name was retained for a while but Stone and Webster employees took over the company's administrative positions and announced that the company planned to build the $6 million project that Biggs and Freeman had proposed. Freeman was out in the cold. His fate is unknown but he had nothing more to do with hydroelectric development on the Skagit.

After 1913, the notices posted along the Upper Skagit were primarily those of Stone and Webster and, using the Skagit Power plans, it obtained a permit to begin construction on the Skagit project. Early in 1914, Stone and Webster obtained additional Forest Service and county permits for work on both the Skagit and Cascade rivers. But construction never started on either project. Stone and Webster also determined that the Skagit was a costly river to tackle and emphasis shifted to the Baker River, which joined the Skagit at Concrete. Stone and Webster had built an electric interurban railroad up the Skagit Valley to Concrete, so work there would be cheaper and the power would have a ready customer. The Skagit Power Co. name was then dropped and Stone and Webster transferred its interest in the Skagit to one of its subsidiaries, the Puget Sound Traction Power and Light Co.

Trolley on the electric interurban railroad up the Skagit Valley to Concrete. Galen Biery Collection, Whatcom Museum of History & Art.

Puget Sound regularly posted its water-right notices on the Skagit, but in 1916 they all expired because no construction had started.

Seattle City Light became interested in developing the river.

City Light had built a hydroelectric project in 1908 on the Cedar River, south of Seattle. The plant was small but it served the city's needs for a few years. When more power was needed, City Light was forced to build a temporary steam plant, but it hardly filled the gap.

James Delmage Ross, 1911

James Delmage Ross, City Light's superintendent, investigated the Skagit in 1912 and 1913 and had tried to buy Skagit

Power Co. but was out-maneuvered by Stone and Webster. City Light then switched its focus to the Sauk River and obtained permits to build a plant. Late in 1915, City Light was in the final stages of applying for the Sauk permits when Ross learned that Stone and Webster's Skagit permits were about to expire. He wrote letters urging the Department of Agriculture not to extend the permits, stating that City Light was ready to develop the river at once. He argued that a city-owned project would be more in the public interest than the private development of the large Boston firm.

But the Stone and Webster Skagit permits were extended a year, until January 1917. City Light proceeded with its preliminary work at the Sauk site but continued to explore other locations. The Sauk also produced bad news. Drilling showed that the riverbed was a mixture of deep gravel and sand, rendering dam construction prohibitively expensive, and those plans were abandoned. Worse yet, it soon was apparent that Stone and Webster had obtained the rights to build on just about every other possible site in the area.

Stone and Webster's actions are understandable in light of practices at the time. It was plain good business to acquire building locations as early as possible. Equally important, however, socialism was a dirty word for capitalists and public ownership was the first cousin of socialism. Stone and Webster was snapping up every probable hydroelectric site, not only as a hedge, but to thwart the potentially troublesome public utility. The demand for electricity was growing and having sources of generation was a matter of survival for both Stone and Webster and City Light. The Forest Service and Department of Agriculture were in the middle. Having decided that the resources of public lands should be used to their fullest by the developer best able to tap them, they now had to decide whether that developer would be from the public or the private sector. The battle lines were clearly drawn.

When Stone and Webster's Skagit permits expired a second time, Ross and City Light were ready. An application was filed for a dam which City Light proposed to build in Diablo Canyon, with a six-mile tunnel to a location near Goodell's old homestead. In September 1917, Ross was in Washington, D.C., pressing City Light's case before Secretary of Agriculture David Houston. He argued that Stone and Webster held more sites than it could possibly develop and was clearly playing the role of dog in the manger. World War I was by then in full swing and Ross pointed out that industry needed electricity and fuel oil, both of which were in short supply. The steam-generating plants used coal or oil, so the Skagit plants would help alleviate both shortages. Ross proposed the immediate construction of an enormous dam at Ruby Creek with an 11-mile tunnel ending at what would be, for those days, an inconceivably large power station near Goodell Creek. The federal officials were clearly impressed and, aware that the Skagit Project could help with the war effort, agreed to let City Light have its try at building the Skagit dams. The award was made December 22, 1917.[3]

Getting the Skagit permit was easy. Now came the hard part – actually building a dam. Ross was so sure that City Light would get the Skagit permit that he already had survey crews out. Ross hoped to build the dam at Ruby Creek, but his engineers argued that it would take too much time and money to finish the job. Drilling the long power tunnel alone would be a remarkable feat. They suggested that a temporary dam, of concrete or even wood, be constructed somewhere near Gorge Creek and that a shorter, two-mile tunnel be drilled from the dam to the proposed

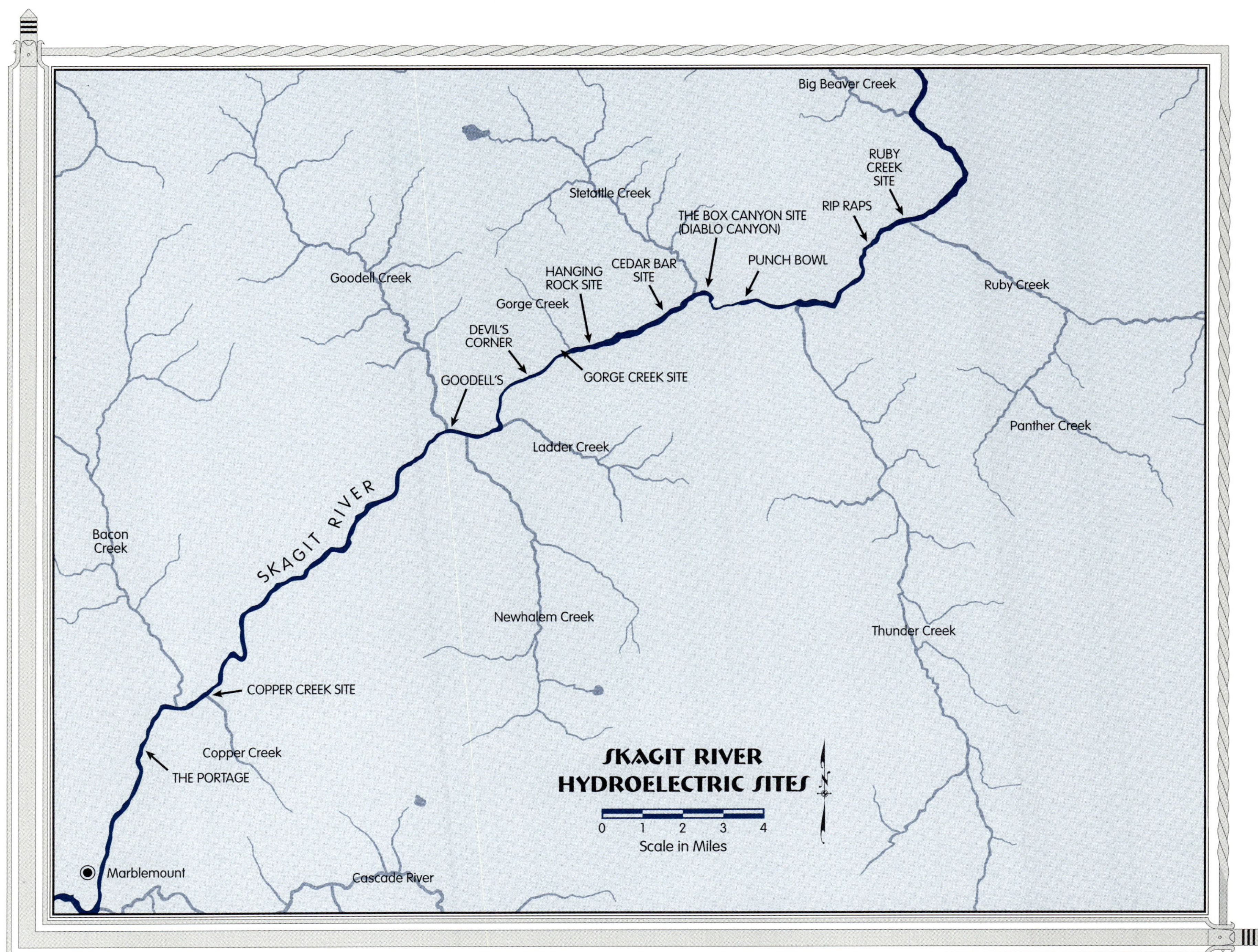
SKAGIT RIVER
HYDROELECTRIC SITES
Big Beaver Creek
RUBY CREEK SITE
RIP RAPS
THE BOX CANYON SITE (DIABLO CANYON)
PUNCH BOWL
Stetattle Creek
CEDAR BAR SITE
HANGING ROCK SITE
Gorge Creek
Goodell Creek
DEVIL'S CORNER
GORGE CREEK SITE
GOODELL'S
Ruby Creek
Panther Creek
Ladder Creek
SKAGIT RIVER
Bacon Creek
Newhalem Creek
Thunder Creek
COPPER CREEK SITE
Copper Creek
THE PORTAGE
Marblemount
Cascade River
0 1 2 3 4
Scale in Miles
N

powerhouse site. After the project was making money, the high dam could be built, the tunnel extended and the job completed.

In early 1918, the Seattle City Council appropriated $5 million for construction of a dam and powerhouse on the Skagit. This demonstrated good faith to the Secretary of Agriculture and work on final approval of City Light's construction permits proceeded.

But when the Forest Service learned of City Light's plans to erect only a temporary dam at Gorge Creek it protested, fearing that might mean construction farther upriver would be delayed or postponed indefinitely. Ross argued that the temporary structure would guarantee that all of the Skagit's potential could be developed. To prove his point, he sent both the Forest Service and the Secretary of Agriculture plans and permit applications for the complete Ruby Creek project. But with the plans was the application for a temporary dam at Gorge Creek.

Proposed Gorge Dam site, 1919. Seattle Municipal Archives

City Light also had some headaches at home. Newspapers in Seattle urged caution, fearing that the project would run Seattle far into debt, that the site was unworkable, expensive, experimental and unnecessary. But Ross was a master politician and he convinced the city council and mayor to see the Skagit first hand. When the tour was over and the arm-twisting completed, the officials were ready to do just about anything Ross asked. What a spellbinder he must have been, as he recounted the many wonderful ways that the Skagit could be exploited. There was a one-dam plan, a two-dam plan and a three-dam plan, all with sets of transmission lines running to Seattle, supported by tall, gleaming steel towers. They might have to settle for wooden poles for a while, but in time the steel was sure to come. Behind each dam would be a lake, around which would flourish scenic alpine resorts, resembling those in Switzerland.

Heady with the fresh air of the Cascades, the officials returned to Seattle and Mayor Ole Hanson became the Skagit's No. 1 booster. Bids on the Gorge Creek project had been sought, but the mayor was startled to find that few contractors would accept Seattle's bonds in payment. In fact, the only firm willing to take on the bonds was also the high bidder. Hanson vowed to sell the Skagit and change their minds. And if a contractor could not be found, the mayor said, the city would take on the job itself. One way or another, the Skagit would be built.[4]

Plans for the Skagit were taking shape. There would be a railroad from Rockport, 25 miles to the Gorge Dam site. When the second dam was built, the lake behind Gorge Dam would provide a convenient highway for barges that would float equipment and crews to the site. But a few more worries were developing. There was speculation, for example, that the Skagit froze over in the winter and that power generation would be limited to the summer months. Then the Department of Agriculture rejected all of City Light's permit applications, stating that insufficient preliminary exploration had been done, and that the project was not yet adequately planned.[5] Furthermore, because of the war, City Light could not sell bonds to finance construction, either by itself or through a contractor. Ross was stopped at every turn. There also were some who feared building a dam on the Skagit might cost more than $5 million.

Pack trail above railroad bridge, 1921.

Exploration work near Gorge Creek continued and City Light crews continued drilling. A private company was hired to substantiate the City's findings and, in addition, a University of Washington geologist was consulted. They all reached the same conclusions. A glacier had once moved down the Skagit, carrying with it tons of gravel and crushed rock. The glacier had ended at about Ruby Creek and when it melted the gravel washed downstream. It was still there in the riverbed, sometimes hundreds of feet deep. Any big dam at Gorge Creek could be built only after the gravel was removed; an expensive proposition, assuming it was even possible.[6]

Exploration work continued and more thought was given to building the first dam at either Diablo Canyon or Ruby Creek. But there were problems at both locations and focus returned to Gorge Creek. By then the war was over and at least it no longer was difficult to sell Seattle's bonds. That was one problem resolved.

A road of sorts was built from Marblemount part way up to the old Goodell homestead and a camp was established, using tents and the buildings left behind by August Dohne and others. Barges loaded with equipment were towed up river, using lines tied around trees along the shore, wound on spools turned by steam engines on the barges. The settlement was called Goodell Creek City and a small sawmill was built, but the primary emphasis was drilling and exploration. The crews had to find bedrock before any dam could be built and it was beginning to appear that the gravel was deeper than even the geologists had thought. One estimate for a high concrete dam, under those circumstances, was more than $30 million, which shook both Ross and city council members to their cores.[7]

City Light had thus far spent $120,000 on preliminary investigations at Gorge Creek and it was beginning to look like money down the drain. Work on the road and sawmill stopped until it could be decided exactly where the dam would be placed. There also was another problem. Postwar inflation rates were

Looking down Diablo River toward foot bridge. Seattle Municipal Archives

soaring and Ross realized that the longer it took to start construction, the more everything would cost. Furthermore, since no actual work had started on a dam, Stone and Webster again was waiting for City Light to show bad faith with the Department of Agriculture, hoping to regain the Skagit as its own. Ross urged fast action to avoid catastrophe. The estimate for the Gorge Creek dam had reached $9 million. The drills were turning full time at Gorge Creek and Ruby Creek but the rock was hard, the river cold and the weather bad. The city council was beginning to wonder when it all would end. Ross decided to build despite the obstacles and convinced the city council to agree to start building at Gorge Creek and hope for the best. He was sure the project would succeed and that the city could afford no further delay.

On September 10, 1919, construction of the Gorge Creek project began. Work also resumed on the road and sawmill and a small, temporary power plant was built on Newhalem Creek. It would supply the electricity necessary for construction of the main dam and powerhouse. But the city council was leery of Ross and insisted that an outside engineer be hired to supervise the work. They chose Carl F. Uhden of Spokane and gave him complete control of the project, which irritated Ross.[8]

Uhden first halted construction of the road to Goodell Creek and reverted, instead, to the original plans that called for a railroad. The city council argued that a road was needed eventually, while the railroad would be useless after the dam was built. But Uhden prevailed and work on the railroad proceeded. Surprisingly, Ross agreed with Uhden.

J.D. Ross never resolved his fear of the private power companies and he always believed they were out to sabotage or in some way undo the Skagit project. He reasoned that a railroad would better limit movement into the project and he even helped Uhden find materials and equipment for the city to buy, including rails that were purchased from the Great Northern. Meanwhile, tracked vehicles and barges were busy hauling equipment up to Goodell Creek.

Generator at Diablo Powerhouse, 1936.

The Mandic Construction Co. was the first contractor to win the Skagit project contract. For $62,000, it said it could build the bed for the railroad from Marblemount to Goodell Creek. Mandic himself believed that the bluffs along the river were either gravel or sandstone. It was quite a shock when he found they were solid granite and a worse shock when he went bankrupt. But he completed most of the job before he went under and City Light crews finished it.[9]

The Grant-Smith Co. of Portland, Ore., laid the track for $500,000. City Light rented locomotives and other equipment from logging companies in the north Cascades. It bought rights-of-way wherever needed and by the end of 1920 work was well under way.

There were no environmental impact studies or conservation groups in those days to challenge projects such as the Skagit dams, but there was some concern for the fish and wildlife. City Light had been told its proposed dam would disrupt the salmon runs. To compensate for the damage, a $10,000 fish hatchery was planned near the proposed Gorge Powerhouse. But later the city and Forest Service agreed that the loss of the salmon run would be inconsequential and hatchery plans were dropped, temporarily at least.[10]

By the end of 1919, there were 100 workers living near Goodell Creek, the sawmill was complete, timber was cut and stockpiled and Goodell Creek was diverted and dammed to form a large mill pond. Some permanent buildings were under construction a short distance upstream. The Forest Service was still considering City Light's final applications for the Gorge Creek plant and assigned A. P. Davis, chief engineer of the Reclamation Service, to work with Uhden and monitor progress. At that point, City Light planned to build a dam 25 feet high near Gorge Creek. From there a tunnel two miles long and 25 feet in diameter would be drilled to the powerhouse site and two generators would be installed. A second tunnel would be added later, plus a third and even a fourth generator. The Ruby Creek project was dropped because of its estimated cost.[11]

As 1920 began, by the time the snow had melted, there were 500 workers on the Skagit project. As the Forest Service, Department of Agriculture and Washington state officials approved City Light's permits, heavy drills and jack hammers were working on the small tunnel for the Newhalem power plant. A small powerhouse was built a few yards from where Newhalem Creek entered the Skagit and a tunnel, 2,650 feet long and almost six feet in diameter, was drilled through the mountain to a point where it intercepted Newhalem Creek. When the tunnel was completed a Westinghouse hydroelectric generating unit was installed, providing 2,500 kilowatts at 6,600 volts. The railroad had been completed and the machinery was brought in on flatcars, hoisted across the river on cables and installed. The water was turned on in August 1921. The "temporary" plant, still there today, had cost slightly more than $800,000.

Skagit River R.R. affectionately known as the "Toonerville Trolley" that meets all the Trains. 1921

Living quarters were being built for the workers and their families and a regular city was appearing on the flat just below the powerhouse site. City Light built 75 three-bedroom cottages and six bunkhouses, a big cookhouse and warehouse next to the railroad track. As more employees moved in, they petitioned Whatcom County for a school. Civilization had arrived at the Upper Skagit.

And religion too. In April 1921, the Bellingham Presbytery sent a logging camp missionary named L.H. Peterson to save souls along the Skagit and he immediately started a newspaper for camp residents. Called "Fits and Starts," the weekly gossip sheet publicized picnics, social events, scriptural messages and not infrequent invitations for those in need of saving to visit the Sunday services.[12]

A town that large needed a name and many thought it should be called Goodell City, like the old tent camp down by the sawmill. During the summer of 1921 a group of college students was hired to work at the project. When it was announced that the city council was due on an inspection tour, the boys grabbed a big plank from the sawmill and painted "Welcome to Newhalem" on it with roofing tar. The name stuck and the settlement has been called Newhalem since.

There were 1,000 residents in Newhalem in 1921 and the lucky ones with houses had electricity, supplied by the small generator at Newhalem Creek. The railroad was being extended to the Gorge Dam site and a bridge was being built at Devil's Elbow. Both because of the name of the old mining trail in there and the sharp curves at each end of the bridge, it was natural that the structure be called the Devil's Elbow Bridge. City Light purchased some World War I surplus equipment for its railroad. First there was a gasoline-powered motor car which could carry 25 passengers called, affectionately, the "Toonerville." Then there was a gasoline freight car, a few flatcars, three electric engines and other equipment. The railroad from Goodell Creek to Gorge Creek was electrified.

On October 24, 1921, the R.C. Storrie Co. of San Francisco was awarded a contract for construction of the Gorge power tunnel. Its bid was just more than $2.25 million. There was a sour note, however, when Ross estimated it might be two years or more before any electricity was generated at Gorge. In 1919, he had said it would take only 18 months to complete the job. Some city council members grumbled and there was considerable comment in the Seattle newspapers but work on the project continued. The Storrie crew built a bunkhouse and started bringing in their equipment. They had a narrow-gauge railroad and decided to add a third rail between the two rails of the city's line and use that, saving both time and money.

The plans called for the power tunnel to be dug from both ends at once. An access tunnel, called the central adit, would be carved into the mountain at the midpoint and work on the tunnel would also be conducted from there. The four headings would be worked at the same time. The central adit was near the Devil's Elbow Bridge and crews had to dig 1,300 feet until they reached the point where the power tunnel would pass. Large electrically powered air compressors were installed in Newhalem and an eight-inch pipe carried the compressed air to the jack hammers two miles away at Gorge, and one mile away at the central adit.

Bench drilling crew and Jumbo, 1923.
Seattle Municipal Archives

In the winter of 1921, floods washed away part of the railroad, which was still not complete. Some of the right-of-way was covered with mud up to 10 feet deep. Then snow slides buried other parts of the line and freezing temperatures slowed work on the power tunnel. When spring came and the flooding ended, work resumed and, in 1922, crews began clearing the route for the transmission lines, stretching from the Skagit almost 100 miles to Seattle. City Light itself built the Gorge Powerhouse, completed in December 1923. Then it started installing the two generators.

With city crews working on the powerhouse, Storrie crews drilling the power tunnel, Grant-Smith finishing the railroad and others felling trees for the transmission lines, an acute power shortage developed and the various supervisors fought among themselves for the electricity that the Newhalem plant was generating. Somehow, the City Light crews always seemed to win, so the powerhouse was completed on time but the power tunnel was far from finished by the end of 1923 and well behind schedule. As if that was not enough, the railroad crew discovered gold along the right-of-way and for a while it was difficult keeping men on the job. When they did return to work, the Storrie crew accidentally touched off a forest fire which not only burned a good deal of the valley but took part of the railroad with it. The Forest Service commandeered all of the men in Newhalem to fight the fire. When it was over the Storrie workforce went out on strike, demanding higher pay and better food in the cookhouse. Their main complaint was the cold lunches they were served. Of course they got cold lunches because there was no power available to do much else. The strike ended 15 days later when the workers were given a 50-cent-a-day raise.

The big problem, however, was the shortage of power. The Storrie Co. was by then well beyond the time limits of its contract and it had agreed to pay City Light $500 for each day that the tunnel remained unfinished. The company blamed the City for the power shortage and the delay and received an extension on its contract. While an eventual legal battle over the contract was shaping up, progress was made on the tunnel. Early in 1924, the transmission lines were nearly complete, the generators were almost ready, the turbines were installed and the power tunnel was going through. During the period of low water, in January and February, work started on the dam itself.

City Light crews built the dam at Gorge Creek. Uhden decided that a concrete dam would be far too expensive and would take too long to complete. He substituted plans for a temporary structure made of logs, a wood crib diversion dam called a weir. It would be high enough to raise the level of the river and divert the flow of water into the power tunnel, and would do until a permanent dam could be built.

But the lower dam meant that the generators could not operate at full capacity. Seattle newspapers jumped on the news and pointed out that the project was years behind schedule, would take at least 12 months more and that it had already cost well over $11 million, with no relief in sight.[13] The newspapers speculated that, by the time the dam was completed and the interest on the bonds paid, the Skagit project would cost a whopping $13 million. The Storrie Co. was working on the third extension of its contract and was unwilling to say when the tunnel would be finished, if ever. Ross was upset, the city council was upset, the mayor was upset and the newspapers had a field day.

The *Seattle Star* blamed Uhden for the delays, claimed that the Skagit was a fiasco and demanded a full investigation. It said

Uhden had purposely prolonged construction to keep his job, which paid $7,800 a year. A Star headline demanded: "Not a Nickel More... until the Skagit Mystery is solved."[14]

But Edwin J. Brown, now the mayor, estimated that the investigation might cost $50,000. He wrote a series of articles in the *Star* detailing all the obstacles that had been encountered on the Skagit and that rising costs everywhere had caused most of the problems. The mayor theorized that there was no mystery about what was happening on the Skagit – a muddle maybe, but certainly no mystery.

The city council fired Carl Uhden in June, however. The luckless engineer had managed to spend the last of the $11 million appropriated by the council and had sought more to finish the project. That was too much and he was sent packing. As if there was not enough trouble, an ex-city employee named Charles Gallant made the headlines with his claim that the Gorge tunnel was so poorly designed that when it was filled with water, there would be a "water hammer" effect. It would be felt and heard miles away, perhaps even in Seattle.[15]

Work was too far along to be stopped at that late date, however. On May 1, 1924, the upper headings of the power tunnel met, and perfectly at that. A few days later the lower headings met and were about an inch off, which was insignificant. The horseshoe-shaped tunnel had only to be lined with concrete and the job would be done. A special gun was developed which shot mixed concrete between wooden forms and the rock walls. By August the work was finished. It had cost $2.5 million.

With the power tunnel completed, the Storrie Co. packed up its middle rail and left the Skagit. The Grant-Smith Co. had already abandoned its camp and most of the tents that surrounded the more permanent buildings disappeared, leaving only the City Light houses. Ross started hiring permanent employees for the project. He sought men who had worked at least a few years for City Light because he was, as always, on guard against "spies" who might be agents for what he called "The Other Company."[16] The first powerhouse superintendent at Gorge was Theodore F. Kane, who had known Ross for years. He got the job when the chief operator at City Light's Cedar Falls plant turned it down, reasoning that the first time there was any high water it would wash the entire project away.

Early in September 1924, the two Gorge Powerhouse generators were tested and there was only one hitch. City Light had installed a telephone system and used the new transmission lines to connect Newhalem with Seattle. The phones were also tied in with the Forest Service network and whenever the Skagit generators were started every phone in the Forest Service and at City Light rang. That problem was quickly solved.

Georgetown steam plant. Seattle Municipal Archives

Work on the timber dam at Gorge Creek continued and special valves, called relief valves, were installed at the central adit so that there would be a way to relieve pressure in the tunnel if a water hammer effect did develop. On September 14, 1924, the first electrical power from the Skagit generators reached Seattle. Three days later there was a formal dedication. As President Calvin Coolidge pressed a gold key in the White House, a spark flashed across the nation over the Postal Telegraph Cable Co.'s wires to the City Light offices in Seattle and then to the Skagit where the signal tripped the generators into operation. At the same time, a whistle at City Light's Lake Union Steam Plant blew, informing the citizens of Seattle that, at last, the Gorge Creek project was delivering power.

In October, work was finished on the dam. One bit of legal business remained; the Storrie Co. claims. Late in 1924 it settled with City Light for $88,824 over its contract price. Ross stated that delays in construction at Gorge cost $500,000 in interest on the bonds which the city had sold. In a final accounting, it was estimated that the dam and powerhouse cost something more than $13 million.

1924 was a landmark year in Upper Skagit history. There now was no doubt how the resources of the valley would be developed or by whom. From 1924 on, the story becomes more a matter of what dam to build next and why.

Chapter 4

Let's Build Another Dam – Somewhere Else

Politics had come to the Upper Skagit story only once in a while to this point, but from 1924 until the start of World War II, politics was the name of the game. To understand the scene, it is as important to follow events in Seattle as it is on the river itself. Seattle City Light's fight to assert itself and withstand the pressure from the competing private power companies was a hard-fought battle. The maneuvering and financial manipulations were not easy to understand.

It also is important to understand what the situation was at Gorge Creek in 1924. There was a dam of sorts, made of logs, diverting the Skagit into a two-mile-long tunnel, ending at a powerhouse with two generators that were small by today's standards. There was a camp and a railroad with a few bridges. Considering what $13 million could buy at that time, the Skagit Project hardly showed why it had cost so much.

The site today is about a 2½-hour drive from Seattle and it appears to be just another small town in the mountains. But in 1924, Newhalem Camp was often isolated, primitive and subject to more than the usual problems that might face settlements in the hills. Just running the generators and transmitting the power to Seattle was often a challenge. A kite string fell across the transmission lines one day and shorted out the entire generating system, blacking out parts of Seattle. Later, pigeons alighted on the wires, again shorting out the system. One conductor broke and fell on a telephone wire which burned and started a forest fire.

In the winter the stream flow did slow, depending on the temperature. If there was a heavy snow and ice, the river nearly dried up. Ross maintained that this reinforced the need to build the remaining dams which would create large lakes with abundant storage for low-water months. In the meantime, the problem was sometimes critical.

With snow came slides and they swept away the trails, parts of the railroad and made life generally difficult. Sometimes the snow was so heavy that it halted the trains. It was not uncommon for Newhalem to be isolated and in January 1925 it was cut off for three weeks.

When there was ice on the river it formed around the power tunnel intake, sometimes blocking the intake entirely. Crews were sent upriver in the freezing cold with picks and axes to chop away the ice.

When the weir at Gorge Creek was built, it was lower than the planned dam and, in an effort to raise the level of the pond behind the dam even a few feet, flashboards were affixed to the top of the dam. They were a series of boards held in place by spring hinges. It

The Skagit River Hotel at Barron. Whatcom County Museum of History & Art

worked, but when the river water velocity increased beyond a certain point, the flashboards fell, one by one, allowing the water to surge past. Crews then had to replace them and it was a difficult job at best.

If the summer was hot, there were forest fires and in 1925 a blaze raced down Bacon Creek, just missing the transmission lines and damaging some City Light equipment. There were more fires in 1926 and 1927. The camp once was on standby for evacuation when a fire threatened, but a timely wind saved the day.

If natural hazards were not bad enough, there was the lingering fear that hostile strangers would infiltrate the work crews and sabotage some of the machinery or the powerhouse. When emery dust was found in the oil that lubricated the generators, Ross openly accused vandals in the employ of what he called "rival companies."

When rocks and sand were found in the axle boxes of City Light locomotives, there were more suspicions but nothing was ever proved. The incidents reinforced Ross' determination not to build the road to Newhalem. The limited access provided by the railroad was enough.

Two men jointly supervised Newhalem Camp. Dana Currier was foreman of the work crews and Theodore Kane managed the powerhouse. Both were close friends of Ross and he trusted them without reservation. It was unfortunate that they had little time for each other. Currier and his crews were often snubbed by Kane and the powerhouse employees, who generally had more education. In the small, isolated town the employees split into two factions. The wives followed suit, dividing into social cliques, each existing only to irritate the other.

The Seattle newspapers picked up on the constant bickering on the Skagit and it was a considerable embarrassment to Ross. When Currier and Kane exchanged a couple of punches, Ross had to step in. Currier, the stronger of the two, became head man on the project and Kane was left with his powerhouse, which he supervised until 1942 when he retired due to ill health.

A school and a few more permanent houses were built at Newhalem Camp and there were bunkhouses for the bachelors. It was a pleasant community, in an isolated way.

The Gorge Creek plant operated well enough, but was primitive by today's standards. The predicted water hammer appeared, but it was hardly felt outside the powerhouse let alone in Seattle. Water in the power tunnel surged irregularly at times, causing rapid pressure fluctuations and changes in the frequency at which the electricity was generated. It could jump from 58 to 62 cycles per second, at an extreme.

Relief valves had been placed in the central adit and when surging occurred, a worker was sent to open them and that usually helped.[2]

At times the Gorge Powerhouse control room was monitoring the entire Seattle electrical system and when its meters were malfunctioning workers often relied on a light bulb. When it appeared dim, operators released more water through the turbines; when it appeared too bright, they slowed the flow. An unusually heavy surge of water in the tunnel or some other problem might produce a surge of electrical power, creating an electrical "bump." In those early years, it was not uncommon to experience two or three bumps daily in Seattle and they were hard on light bulbs and electric motors.

All this further convinced Ross that City Light had to build another Skagit dam and the sooner the better. The question was, where? Diablo? Ruby? They were both good sites and others were suggested by city council members. Some of them liked a site called Hanging Rock, just upstream from Gorge Creek.

In September 1924, even before the Gorge plant was formally dedicated, Ross filed for permits on the Diablo and Ruby locations. But city council members said the Gorge Creek permanent concrete dam should be built first, arguing that it would be better to finish one project before starting a second.

But Ross countered that a bigger dam with greater water storage could be built farther upstream, providing both a new powerhouse and a constant water flow at the Gorge plant. Then, as if on command, the Skagit River flooded, causing considerable damage downstream on the Skagit Flats. The city council then got carried away and considered building a big dam on Ruby Creek, for both power and flood control. Over the objections of both Ross and Mayor Brown, the city council allocated $8 million for construction of the Ruby Creek plant.[3]

A few weeks later, cooler heads prevailed and the council decided, over the mayor's objections, to send a team of experts to the Skagit to determine the best place to build. While the experts hiked up and down the river, costing the city $12,000, Ross had his own team studying the problem and they discovered that, before anything could be built at Ruby Creek, the railroad would have to be extended nine miles upriver. The roadbed would be over steep, unfriendly ground and the lowest cost estimate was more than $1 million. That ended serious thought of building at Ruby Creek.[4]

Diablo Canyon appeared to be the best location for a second Skagit dam. The railroad would have to be extended about five miles, but that was simple enough. And once there was a dam at Diablo the lake behind it could be used to barge material to the Ruby site. Ross also urged installation of a third generator in the Gorge Powerhouse, then called the Ross Powerhouse.[5]

Early in 1926, City Light applied for permits for its site at Diablo and drilling was started there, seeking bedrock and the best location for the dam. Work started on the railroad in June and City Light initiated proceedings to acquire the Davis ranch. By September it was fairly certain that the dam would be built at the lower end of Diablo Canyon, with the powerhouse around the bend in the river, against the west side of Sourdough Mountain. Ross, heady with success, confidently predicted that by 1950 the Skagit would be completely tamed by three great dams.

City Light had approved the final plans for the design of Diablo Dam by mid-1927 and Maj. W. Chester Morse of Seattle had been appointed to supervise construction. Morse immediately requested $85,000 to begin building the tunnel that would divert water from the dam site and, to everyone's surprise, the city council refused to appropriate the money. Council members remembered that the Gorge project had been built piecemeal and they decided that, at Diablo, they would offer the entire project for bid, hiring one contractor for everything. The council member most opposed to the Skagit project was Oliver T. Erickson, who had been suspicious of both Ross and the project. He maintained that Gorge Creek was poorly planned and that Diablo would be more of the same.

The railroad extension was complete except for a funicular incline hoist, necessary to raise the flatcars and equipment the last 300 feet up the mountain. The Washington Iron Works of Seattle started working on the lift at a cost of $21,418 and when it was completed work on the dam could begin.

While the city council debated building at Diablo, the roof fell in. It was the roof of the Gorge tunnel intake and it had been a trouble spot since the project began operation. From the start, large amounts of gravel managed to enter the tunnel and damage machinery in the powerhouse. When the plan to build a high concrete dam at Gorge was abandoned in favor of the lower, temporary wood weir, the augmented design for the power tunnel entrance was a Rube Goldberg affair that proved poor at best. There were proposals on how to correct the situation but they all involved thousands of dollars with no guarantee of success.

Workers pose on the Diablo incline lift.

City Light crews laid a concrete floor along part of the river bottom near the power tunnel entrance early in 1927, hoping that it would stem the flow of gravel but it was only a partial success. Work around the intake was costing more than $6,000 a day and city council members began to believe that perhaps they should complete the Gorge project before proceeding with Diablo.

One plan that became popular with some city council members involved building a high dam at Hanging Rock, a short distance upstream from Gorge Creek. The gravel there was shallower than at the Gorge site and, after extending the existing tunnel and adding two or three more units at Gorge, the city would have a complete project, minus the intake problem.

When the intake entrance collapsed and Ross asked the city council for $250,000 to replace the wood dam with a temporary concrete structure, the fat was in the fire. Erickson maintained Ross was throwing good money after bad and that the best bet was to build at Hanging Rock. In November, Erickson managed to talk the council into allocating $100,000 for extensive exploration at Hanging Rock.

Ross was horrified. Any construction at Hanging Rock would flood the railroad to Diablo, which was already built. Worse yet, if a large dam was constructed at either Gorge or Hanging Rock, the valley would be blocked in such a way that travel to the upriver sites would be difficult, if not impossible. Ross lobbied hard and wrung from a majority of the council permission to proceed with work at Diablo, although consideration was also to be given to the Hanging Rock plan. [6]

City Light took bids on the dam at Diablo and awarded the job to the Winston Brothers Construction Co. of Minneapolis, Minn., for $2,362,738.[7] By December, work was well under way on the diversion tunnel and, much to everyone's surprise, the city council approved all the necessary contracts.

Outmaneuvered but not finished, Erickson then introduced an ordinance allocating $8 million to complete work at Diablo, add the third generator at Gorge and build a dam at Hanging Rock. Ross again spent considerable time lobbying sympathetic council members and when Erickson was in California on a business trip, the council passed an ordinance indefinitely postponing all Hanging Rock plans.[8]

When he returned to Seattle, Erickson was furious and insisted that the Hanging Rock site be reconsidered. He argued that both the Diablo and Hanging Rock dams should be built at the same time, which Ross felt could drive City Light so deeply into debt that the still-infant utility might default or even go bankrupt. Erickson convinced the council to view the two sites first hand, accompanied by a friend who worked for a construction company that was interested in building the Hanging Rock Dam.

Now it was Ross with his back against the wall and he told the press that the city should concentrate on the Diablo project, which already was well under way. There would be ample time later to build another dam. Erickson, back from the Skagit with the council, urged that bids be sought on the Hanging Rock Dam. Each side provided the newspapers with experts who said the Hanging Rock adventure would either save or sink City Light.

An ordinance budgeting money for a powerhouse at Diablo was defeated and the debate appeared to be a standoff. The Seattle Municipal League then joined the controversy and undertook a six-week study of the issue. In January 1928, it opposed the Hanging Rock project and, with the League's report in his pocket, Ross effectively undercut Erickson. For a while the Hanging Rock issue faded from view.[9]

Work was moving slowly at Diablo. The diversion tunnel was almost completed and by midsummer crews were working on the dam itself. Another crew was clearing timber and brush from the area where Diablo Lake would rise. There was a setback when the Skagit flooded, washed away some coffer dams and inundated the construction site. A second flood in the fall carried away another coffer dam, some pumps and other equipment. Work on the dam was stopped for more than a month. But the dam at Diablo was taking shape almost on schedule.

It also was obvious that a powerhouse would have to be built at Diablo. The city council already had rejected one appropriation for such a structure and, early in 1928, it voted against a second proposal. In June, City Light requested $3 million for work on the Diablo Powerhouse. It was the opening that Erickson was awaiting. Until then, Mayor Bertha Landes had usually voted against Erickson, but Landes no longer was mayor. Frank Edwards had been elected to the post and he, along with Erickson, favored reconsideration of the old Hanging Rock project. Whenever Ross tried to obtain money for work at Diablo, Erickson and Edwards tied the request to plans for work at Hanging Rock. But they did agree on the third generator at Gorge and, late in 1928, the necessary money was appropriated. The generator was installed and running a year later.

The battles between city council members and Ross raged through 1928 and into 1929. In a clever maneuver, Erickson managed an order to rehabilitate the railroad and cut 75 workers from the Skagit workforce. Work stopped temporarily at Diablo but Ross alerted the council and within a few days the council voted to rehire them. Then, as if tired of the whole matter, the council allocated $50,000 to rebuild the small dam at Gorge Creek. By

A triptych of Diablo.

the end of 1929 the money had been spent on new flashboards and a few other features.[10]

There was good news and bad news in 1930. The good news was that the Hanging Rock issue appeared dead. The bad news was that the Great Depression had struck and money for any construction project was hard to find. The Diablo Powerhouse had to be financed somehow and it appeared that would be no easy matter.

Ross first investigated buying generators. The original plans called for three dams on the Skagit with six uniform generators at each location. But Ross was an innovator. He read scientific magazines that speculated generators much larger than those in common use could be successfully built and operated. He dreamed of having the biggest generators in the world on the Skagit and he boldly proposed that City Light order two super-sized, 60,000 kilowatt units for the Diablo Powerhouse.[11]

Lesser minds boggled when they heard Ross expound on the magnificent giants that would be the pride of City Light's project. The inflation of the 1920s had driven prices up and by 1930 the Skagit had already set Seattle back more than $74 million. Many believed the entire project was getting out of hand.

Imprudent though it may have appeared, Ross won the generator issue and plans were drawn for a powerhouse to contain the outsized machines. Then Ross had another idea. Rather than building a conventional powerhouse, the Diablo generators would sit on large concrete pedestals. As Ross pointed out, thousands of tourists would see the machines and be impressed by their enormous size, instilling in them even more confidence in City Light.[12] Whatever else he was, James Delmage Ross was a master showman and throughout his planning on the Skagit he always was focused on public relations.

Plans for the Diablo Powerhouse progressed and they even included an elaborate visitors gallery and a tiled goldfish pond. Work started on the power tunnel from the nearly completed dam to the powerhouse. Water had been accumulating behind Diablo Dam since October 1929 and the storage already was being used to even the flow into the Gorge plant.[13] The lake behind Diablo Dam was more than 100 feet deep and rising.

Equipment for the Diablo Powerhouse was ordered early in 1930, including the massive turbines necessary to turn the generators and other gear, such as valves, gates and pipe. By March the power tunnel was complete and the dam itself was almost complete. Diablo Dam was formally dedicated Aug. 27, 1930, with ceremonies on the dam, speeches from flag-draped platforms, ribbons, strings of serpentine everywhere and a band playing patriotic music. The guests enjoyed a big meal in the Winston Brothers cookhouse and a good time was had by all.[14]

It was the highest dam then standing anywhere in the world and to complete it, the incline had hoisted some 1.75 million bags of cement up the mountain in just more than 10,000 trips. It was all wonderful, except for one little snag. The powerhouse was not even operating and finding money was more and more difficult. A contract was let for the powerhouse foundation, but the winning bidder went broke and a second firm had to complete the work.

Then, for almost four years, all work stopped on the Diablo project.

At the same time, City Light was actively competing with Puget Sound Power and Light Company and the apparent success of the Skagit project made the private power interests more apprehensive about City Light's public power challenge. There was big money at stake and in an effort to thwart City Light, powerful private interests frequently pulled political strings. They supported Mayor Edwards and Erickson and generously rewarded those who favored their cause. With advertising money to spend or withhold, they discouraged newspapers from siding with City Light and against them and they were happy to foment any trouble they could for Ross.

Sometimes playing into the hands of private power advocates, the expansive Ross was vulnerable to charges that he wasted money, and public money at that. He pushed costly Skagit construction and experimented with innovative technology. The only brake on Ross' plans was in the hands of Seattle's Engineering Department which was controlled by the city council and not City Light. Ross continually lobbied for an engineering department independent of the council and under his own control. His incessant lobbying, coupled with the popularity he enjoyed with Seattle citizens, galled his adversaries.

The Depression, the costly Diablo construction with its unorthodox generators and the political infighting brought the issue to a boil. It started with charges in the *Seattle Times* that the Diablo power tunnel was too small for the big generators and that in planning the Diablo plant, Ross had contradicted the advice of every competent engineer around. Ross challenged the charges and claimed they were promoted by agents of the private power companies. Ross then arranged for a measure to appear on the upcoming March election ballot that would grant him, as superintendent of lighting, control of all engineering and construction work needed by City Light. It was the last straw. One day before the election, on March 9, 1931, Edwards fired J.D. Ross.[15]

Officials pose at an open penstock gate.

Morse was appointed to replace Ross, who moved with his wife, Alice, to New York, where he served as an adviser to then-Gov. Franklin D. Roosevelt. In Seattle, a drive was launched to recall Edwards and rehire Ross. It was led by liberal attorney Marion A. Zioncheck, who later had an unusual career in Congress. Edwards campaigned hard but the special election, held in July, recalled the mayor in an amazing, 125,000-to-15,000-vote landslide.[16] The new mayor, Robert Harlin, restored Ross as superintendent. In the earlier March election, as a bonus, the voters approved formation of City Light's own engineering department. It was a landmark in City Light history. Never again would private power seriously challenge City Light's existence or its control of the Skagit.

The triumph made Ross both a local and national hero, but the success was diminished by the unavoidable realization that Seattle was unable to sell its bonds in 1931 and that the Diablo project stood unfinished. The giant generators sat on Reflector Bar in special Quonset-type buildings that were air-conditioned to protect them until they could be installed.

There was unusually heavy rainfall on the Skagit that winter and flooding in the valley. Rock and mud slides blocked the railroad and heavy debris piled up against Gorge Dam. There was damage to the weir itself as water poured over the top of the structure and inundated the valley, washing away a good deal of Mount Vernon.[17] City Light was urged to move quickly with its plans to dam and tame the still-wild river.

In an attempt to raise money, Ross asked the federal Reconstruction Finance Corporation for more than $7 million. RFC members even visited the Skagit but the loan application was rejected. Ross was back at the RFC's door in 1933 with expanded plans to build not only the Diablo Powerhouse but to start work at Ruby Creek. At the same time, Franklin Roosevelt became the new president and his measures to counter the Depression were beginning to take shape. One was the National Industrial Recovery Act, designed to increase employment by sponsoring public works that would hire large numbers of workers.[18]

Ross rushed to Washington and made the first application for NIRA funds. Work at Ruby would require 2,000 to 3,000 workers alone to clear the reservoir. With no hesitation, Ross asked the Public Works Administration, an NIRA subsidiary, for more than $18 million.[19] He later increased the request to more than $25 million. With that much money, he could finish Diablo and begin the Ruby Creek project.

But the wheels of the government turned slowly and, while Ross fussed and planned, officials in Washington deliberated. Anticipating the money, Ross convinced the city council to approve ordinances creating the Ruby project and secured property that the third Skagit dam would flood, including 5,491 acres in Canada. The federal government could spend only so much money in any one state and when it budgeted Washington state's entire $64 million allotment for building the massive Grand Coulee Dam on the Columbia River, it also rejected City Light's requests.

Diablo Powerhouse.

The federal government, however, did not overlook the Skagit entirely. A Civilian Conservation Corps camp was built at Bacon Creek where 200 workers were assigned to road and trail construction. The Whatcom Primitive Forest Area was created at the same time and, in 1934, the North Cascade Primitive Area was added, limiting the encroachment of civilization. It was a taste of things to come as government officials and citizens began to question the unfettered development of their natural resources and the disruption of Nature wherever it pleased society to build something.

With hope of obtaining federal money ended, Seattle again tried to sell some of its bonds, and in May 1934 the city managed to sell almost $5 million worth, enough to finish Diablo and construct a new City Light Building in downtown Seattle. With his own engineering department, Ross decided that City Light itself would install the Diablo generators. The John Rumsey Co. was awarded the contract to build the Diablo Powerhouse and work was under way through 1935. Testing began on the first of the two generators Sept. 22, 1936, and on Oct. 5 it was delivering electricity to Seattle.[20] The Third World Power Conference was held in the United States that same month and a special train carried conference delegates on an unusual tour of the Skagit project. At Diablo they witnessed the initial, formal run of what was then the world's largest operating hydroelectric generator. At his Hyde Park home, Roosevelt pressed a switch to start the generator. City Light had the distinction of completing one of the larger heavy construction projects in the United States, during the Depression, without any federal financing.

In early 1937, the second Diablo generator was operating, without fanfare. By the end of the year, all testing on the units was completed and they were providing a steady flow of power for Seattle homes and factories. For the first time since the end of World War I, the Lake Union steam plant was deactivated. The future was looking brighter at the Skagit, where work already had started on the capstone of the Skagit development, the high dam at Ruby Creek.

Chapter 5

Step Right This Way, Folks

The North Cascades must be seen to be fully appreciated. Sharp rock peaks rise against the sky, soaring above steep green alpine valleys. The lakes and the river are the color of a perfect emerald because they contain Skagit gneiss which was ground to a fine powder by the glaciers. The mountain air is clear and cool, especially in the mornings. It is the place of poets and dreamers.

Those who worked in the picture-postcard settings of the Upper Skagit used the scenery to promote the valley. As early as the 1880s, prospective mining investors and prominent citizens were frequently escorted up to the diggings, and as they reveled in the glories of nature, their money was loosened from their pockets and spirited away, like taking candy from preoccupied babies. The Skagit Power Co. and its successor, the Puget Sound Power and Light Co., continued the yearly parade of VIPs, showing off the trees, the hills, the powerful wild river and impressing people of influence with the unlimited possibilities of the untamed Skagit.

Then, with Seattle City Light came the P.T. Barnum of the Northwest, J.D. Ross. Again and again the enthusiastic superintendent of lighting led mayors and city council members over the trails of the Upper Skagit. As they camped along the river, Ross painted pictures of the giant power project that would build Seattle. Ross proselytized, cajoled, convinced, and when his guests were overwhelmed by the majesty and potential of it all, intoxicated by the smell of Douglas fir and visions of limitless electric power, Ross led them back to Seattle where they showed their appreciation by backing the Skagit development to the limit. It happened to Mayor Ole Hanson in 1918, and he was only the first of many.

Tourists line up at Diablo.

But those tours were special events, limited to special guests. The valley was isolated and it was hard to transport many visitors to the area at one time. The first public tour was organized by the Seattle Municipal League and it began June 19, 1922. At six a.m. a car caravan left Seattle, transporting 43 visitors to Rockport where they boarded the train to the Gorge weir, which was still under construction. It was a three-day trip and the highlight was Ladder Creek Falls, a spectacular natural waterfall behind the Gorge Powerhouse.

Later in 1922 and again in 1923 other groups made the trip, but most were professional organizations. In 1924, after the Gorge Powerhouse was in operation, City Light offered a series of one-day excursions to the Skagit at a cost of $7.50 per person. Enough patrons bought tickets to fill six parties of 40 each.[1]

Ross saw the potential for a regular tour, to let Seattle citizens see what they were buying, a painless way to publicize the merits of the Skagit. A more elaborate tour was planned for 1925 and the town of Newhalem was made ready. The old bunkhouses were painted and renovated to accommodate overnight guests. Trails were built through the Ladder Creek area and the Gorge Cookhouse was equipped to feed tourists. A pleasant day and a half trip was planned. Meanwhile, the irregular tours continued.

1926 was the big year. The first guests to try the new ritualized Skagit Tour were 27 women from a women's civic organization. They drove to Rockport, boarded the train to Newhalem, stayed overnight in the bunkhouses, viewed Gorge Dam, Gorge Powerhouse and Ladder Creek the next morning, ate three meals in the cookhouse and were back in Rockport the following afternoon.

The women of Newhalem, wives of City Light employees, were encouraged to improve the gardens around the Gorge Powerhouse and at Ladder Creek. Ross was envisioning a fairyland tourist park on the Skagit. He was given permission by the Forest Service in

1929 to develop Ladder Creek any way he wished. There already were orchids planted along the paths that led to the falls and colored lights illuminated the trails at night. Tour groups wandered through the area in the evenings. In 1929, 2,000 visitors toured the project at a cost of $5 a person.[2]

The tour season was extended from April through November in 1930, with 150 visitors in each group. The tour was expanded to include a visit to Diablo with a ride up the incline hoist and a view of the new dam.

In 1931, each tour had accommodations for 260 visitors and there were three or four groups on the Skagit each week. By 1935, the capacity of the tour had grown to 500, at a cost of $3 a person. Housing was expanded and included platform tents in addition to the bunkhouses.

Lunch for doe at zoo.

Ross had many ideas for improving the Skagit and the tour. When Diablo Dam was completed, he suggested adding barges that would carry 50 to 75 tourists to the Ruby project site. By 1931 a tugboat and barge were transporting tourists, one group at a time, up the lake to see where the next Skagit dam would be built. Ross hired Edward W. Kemoe to manage the tours. A bridge was built across the Skagit near the Gorge cookhouse so tourists could cross the river and see the small Newhalem power plant.

In 1932, J.D. Ross, well ahead of his time, proposed that the federal government create a national park on the Skagit, focusing on the tour and the Ladder Creek area. When the Ruby Creek Dam was built, he said, the 25-mile lake that it created could be illuminated by hundreds, perhaps thousands, of colored floodlights. Vacationers could build summer guest houses along the shores and the slopes above what would certainly become a spectacular resort area. The government rejected the plan.[3]

Ross continued adding to the Ladder Creek area and every year after 1930 more colored lights were added to illuminate the falls each night. By the mid 1930s, it offered spectacular alternating color displays highlighting the natural stair-step falls. Along the trails, strolling tourists could enjoy tropical and domestic plants. During the winter, the more fragile trees and bushes were taken to the powerhouse, then replanted outside after the last spring frosts. Pools were added along the paths, stocked with trout and goldfish. Music drifted through the gardens from hidden speakers. Ross himself picked the records to be played, with an ear toward achieving just the right mood.

Ross also had a zoo of sorts at Diablo, built around a collection of domestic and foreign animals. The menagerie included black squirrels from Mexico, pheasants, mountain sheep, an albino deer, nine cockateels, six African love birds and, at its peak, more than

J.D. and Alice Ross

150 birds and animals. Friends and acquaintances around the country sent animals to Ross for his zoo, as well as cuttings and seeds for the gardens. Ross paid many of the costs out of his own pocket. At some expense, City Light did build a summer retreat cabin at Diablo for Ross and his wife (they had no children), but he only saw it once, in 1937, and never set foot near it again.

The Department of Agriculture contributed 200 Chinese chestnut trees, to be planted on the project as an experiment, but most of them died. A banana tree was imported and it amazed visitors for a few seasons, but the northern climate was too harsh and it eventually died too. Ross dreamed of stripping the hillside behind the Gorge Powerhouse and planting 5,000 rhododendrons and 5,000 pink dogwood trees. He wanted to line the cliffs above the project with 10,000 flowering Japanese cherry trees and an assortment of lilacs, clematis, wisteria and azaleas. But these grandiose plans were never realized.[4]

Ross ordered construction of a large excursion boat to replace the tourist barges, using City Light's small shipyard on Diablo Lake. It was launched in time for the 1937 tour season and was named the Alice Ross. The vessel was powered by a gas engine and carried about 275 tourists. Large, white and luxurious the Alice made two trips up Diablo Lake for each tour (when there was a full complement of 500). On the return from the Ruby site, as the boat cruised into the wide part of the lake, the engine was turned off and, as the tourists drifted slowly along, music from

The Alice Ross launched in time for the 1937 tourist season.

hidden shoreside speakers wafted across the water, enchanting everyone.

At Diablo Dam, the spillways were opened whenever possible, presenting a spectacular cascade of water into the narrow canyon. At the Gorge cookhouse, expansive meals were served and tourists often were given extra pies to take home as souvenirs.[5] In 1934, the price of the tour was $2.50 and about 800 visitors toured the Skagit each week. By 1937, up to 1,500 people took the trip each week and the cost rose to $4.05, which was still a bargain. It must have been because 21,000 tourists visited the project that year.

Ross died in March 1939 and was buried across the river from the Gorge Powerhouse at the base of Goodell Mountain, which was renamed Ross Mountain. The crypt, sealed October 3, 1939, was surrounded with flowering Japanese cherry trees, sent from the White House by Roosevelt. Ross had worked in his last years for Roosevelt as the first director of the Bonneville Power Administration. The Ruby project, then well under way, was renamed the Ross project.

In 1940, the Skagit tour reached its high point and was truly an elaborate production. The trips sometimes started at the King Street Station in Seattle, where visitors boarded the train for Rockport and then for Newhalem. But tourists more often drove their own cars to Rockport, where they were served coffee or tea and walked through floral gardens near the railroad station while waiting for the train. The trip to Newhalem took about an hour and, weather permitting, open gondolas were used, affording views of the scenery in the narrow canyon. At Newhalem, the tourists were assigned to their dormitories, with men in one group and women in the other. Complications not infrequently arose when mischievous Seattleites, familiar with the tour routine, encouraged unsuspecting newlyweds to take the trip as an inexpensive honeymoon. What a shock that must have been, although, as one old-timer reminisced, "There were ways around it, if you were clever enough."

Baggage stored, the guests were taken across the swinging bridge to view the

Newhalem power plant and told it had been the first unit to provide electricity when the project began. They then returned to the cookhouse for dinner. It was served family style and usually included two varieties of meat, vegetables, rolls, pies and ice cream. And this during the Depression.

After dinner, there was a short rest and films were shown in the meeting hall (a converted barn) near the cookhouse. At night the group was escorted along a garden walk past the Gorge Powerhouse to the Ladder Creek Falls area. They toured the powerhouse and were given information about the generators, such as the fact that each one could power 176,000 washing machines or 33,000 electric ranges. It was a soft sell for the virtues of electric power. Then it was off to see the falls and hear "The Waters of the Minnetonka" or "Hark! Hark! My Soul," two of Ross' favorite pieces that he felt most appropriate for the setting. If someone on the tour was confined to a wheelchair, Kemoe and other guides carried them through the gardens and up the steep trail to the falls. When the tour was finished, it was back to the meeting hall for a dance that lasted well into the night.

Soft music drifted through Newhalem Camp to lull guests to sleep but at an early 6 a.m. the guests were jolted awake by the blaring notes of "Lazy Mary, Won't You Get Up?" Breakfast was served at the cookhouse at 7:30, after which the electric train took them to Diablo, stopping to view Gorge Dam along the way.

At Diablo tourists visited the zoo and rode up the mountain on the incline lift. They walked a quarter mile to a viewpoint where they saw Diablo Dam and then on to the dock behind the dam where the Alice Ross was waiting. After they viewed the Ruby-Ross project, they returned and heard more music as they cruised. They returned to Newhalem in time for lunch, packed and then boarded the train for the return to Rockport. When they arrived they found that their cars had been washed and serviced by City Light employees. It was a great finish to a wonderful trip. And it was a pity that, in its final form, the tour was offered only two years. The old Skagit tour was discontinued after 1941 for security reasons, as World War II loomed.

In 1941, 15,877 Seattleites and their friends took the Skagit tour and, from the beginning, more than 100,000 tourists visited the Upper Skagit. Surprisingly, the tour was never advertised, yet after the first year there were seldom empty seats. Small wonder that those old enough to have taken the trip remember it so fondly today.

After the war ended, so much construction was under way along the Upper Skagit that it was not possible to immediately resume the tours. But customers kept asking about them and finally, in 1953, City Light announced that a series of abbreviated one-day trips would be offered. Small groups of 90 or less could take the trips, starting in mid-July and running through Labor Day. What a disappointment that adventure must have been to those who remembered the old tour. The gardens had not been maintained and the zoo in Diablo was gone. The road had been extended to Newhalem and the romance of the train ride also was gone. The Alice Ross was stripped of anything usable in 1948 and the hulk was burned and sunk in the middle of Diablo Lake.

In 1954, the railway between Newhalem and Diablo was removed and tours had to be planned around the schedules of the crews who were dismantling the track. In 1955, there were no tours at all. The tours were resumed in 1956 with a maximum of 50 tourists at a time. The visitors drove to Newhalem, were bused to Diablo and ferried by boats to the Ross Powerhouse construction site. They then walked through the Ladder Creek area to see the falls and the few hardy plants that remained. Alice Maud Wilson Ross died that year and was buried beside her husband, J.D.

In 1958, there were two tours daily with 65 tourists each. City Light bought a surplus Navy vessel that year and trucked it to the Skagit. There was a problem when it was stuck in one of the tunnels on the road. It was refurbished into a new tour boat, the Alice Ross II. The little blue boat carried 100 guests and the tour capacity was increased so that each group just filled the boat. The tours have been offered every year since 1959, except for a two-week interruption in 1963 when heavy construction was under way on the highway. There were three tours daily in 1964 and, after 1967, there were five, from early June through Labor Day. Since 1975, the tour has been shortened so that it starts in Diablo and the traditional meal is served in a new facility there. The tour has been reduced to a matter of hours and there are many each day.

In the early 1960s, after some research, restoration of the Ladder Creek lighting began, and the falls now are illuminated nightly during the summer. But the regular tours do not include a visit to the falls and tourists miss this attractive site unless they visit it themselves.

The original Skagit tour is gone. Today, since the completion of the North Cascades Highway and inclusion of the Upper Skagit in the Ross Lake National Recreation Area, it is possible for people to drive through the project in a matter of minutes, past Ross Dam and into Eastern Washington. But the memory of the old trip lingers, for it had a charm that those who took it will never forget.

Site where hydraulic mining has been operated on the Skagit River, 1901
Darius Kinsey Collection, Whatcom Museum of History & Art.

Chapter 6

Gold! Again?

The impression might have been created that after the power companies started developing the hydroelectric potential of the Skagit not much else occurred in the valley. Nothing could be further from the truth. It is a fact of human history that once gold is discovered, there will always be a few men willing to spend countless hours working under the worst conditions to find it. They are driven by the thought that they might beat the odds and discover what everyone else had missed – a new mine that would bring them fantastic riches.

The problem that had always plagued the miners of the Upper Skagit was the difficulty in getting there. But after City Light built its railroad, first to Gorge Creek and then to Diablo, new hope germinated in the hearts of the men who held claims along the upper reaches of the river. In 1920, the Thunder Creek Mining Co. announced plans to build a monorail road from Gorge Creek to it's holdings on Thunder Creek. While there always had been a few miners working claims in the mountains, 1920 saw an unusual influx of prospectors. But the boom fizzled as fast as it came and the bad weather, along with the post-World War I depression, ended serious activity for the time being.

When the railroad reached Diablo, the mining community was agog again, seeing the long-awaited Skagit boom just around the corner. A group of investors called the Cascade Mineral Corp. bought out many of the mines along Thunder Creek and planned to begin work at some of their holdings, including the site of the old Skagit Queen. They drew plans for a road from Diablo Dam to their mines but the only real work was on paper. Those involved lost their stakes as the Great Depression of the early 1930s finished off this latest group of speculators.

In 1934, two events finally touched off the real mineral rush, such as it was. First, the American Smelting Co. of Tacoma, owned by the Guggenheim family, bought the Azurite Gold Co.'s holdings at Thunder Creek. It announced plans to invest $400,000 for a road from Diablo to the claim.[1] There were so many men out of work that the thought of easy money, or even a job, always drew a crowd. Then, when a miner arrived in Concrete with $30,000 worth of gold from his diggings on Ruby Creek, wise folks got out of the way before they were trampled by the hopeful mob that raced off to strike it rich. Suddenly, there was mining activity again, both at Ruby Creek and Thunder Creek.

The Depression left the mining companies cautious and, because money was tight, they had to seek ways to finance their ventures. The Azurite Co. postponed plans to build a road, hoping to interest the CCC crews to build it for free. The Gold HUI Co., which was active at Ruby Creek, applied to different federal agencies, hoping for money to back its proposals. They bought equipment and hired an engineer to survey a road to their claim, but their requests for money were repeatedly rejected.

Skagit miners. Darius Kinsey Collection, Whatcom Museum of History & Art

On paper, more mines and claims were created, including the Geneva Prospect, the Glory Hole and the Nigger Head. Samples showed the value of the ore to range from $2.10 to 45 cents a ton for gold and an even $2 a ton for silver. At that, mining might pay if there was a cheap way to move the rock out of the isolated upper valley.

Late in 1935 and into 1936, the transportation focus at the mines shifted from bringing a road from the west to bringing it in from the east. There had been an old wagon road over that route 30 or 40 years before and, while it was overgrown and largely washed away, the miners began considering that option. The mining companies applied to the PWA for $125,000 to build the road. They were turned down.

So the mining companies decided to build the road themselves and work began, crossing Hart's Pass and moving west. Optimistic miners actually dismantled automobiles and carried them over the trails, reassembling them at the mining sites, where they waited for the arrival of the road.[2]

By mid-1936, a dozen or more mines were in operation. At Gold Hill, gasoline cost an unheard of 85 cents a gallon and other goods ran 25 cents a pound more than their usual price. But the miners had 10 tons of partly refined ore ready to ship, the money would be rolling in and everyone was happy. On Thunder Creek, 40 miners were working full-time at the Azurite and more were employed next door at the Mammoth mines. The Azurite had imported a cyanide gold ore reduction mill and other expensive equipment.

Ross Dam under construction. Seattle Municipal Archives

In 1937, the Forest Service gave the miners a spiritual boost. It suggested that the Bureau of Public Roads and Forest Service jointly finish the road, eventually connecting to City Light's project and completing the long-discussed cross-state highway.[3] In 1938, Whatcom County allocated $25,000 for construction of a link in the road that would stretch from the Ruby Dam site up Ruby Creek to Canyon Creek where it would meet the road from the east. The county spent about $5,000 for the road survey, but became wary and no additional money was forthcoming. The county and the Forest Service tried to obtain funds from the WPA but the applications were denied.

Surprisingly enough, the Azurite mines started to show a little profit and, in 1938, 65 miners were working there. The companies invested more money in the road and some work was completed along Ruby Creek.

When the North Cascade Wilderness Area was created in 1934, the Forest Service, its awareness of conservation and resource protection still limited, had halted all road building until the effect of such construction could be determined. But the miners quickly resumed work and they assumed they would be exempt from the new government restrictions. There was always the nagging fear, however, that conservationists might stop mining altogether. Furthermore, Glenn Smith, assistant superintendent for City Light, pointed out that when the Ruby Creek Dam was completed, it would flood part of the planned road.[4] It was time to reconsider.

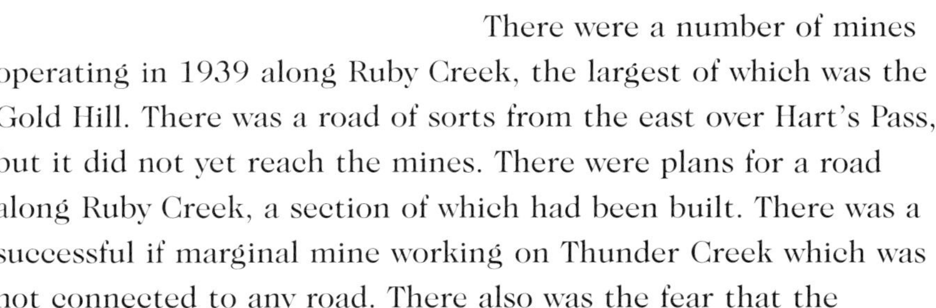

There were a number of mines operating in 1939 along Ruby Creek, the largest of which was the Gold Hill. There was a road of sorts from the east over Hart's Pass, but it did not yet reach the mines. There were plans for a road along Ruby Creek, a section of which had been built. There was a successful if marginal mine working on Thunder Creek which was not connected to any road. There also was the fear that the government would further restrict activity in the area, making all mining difficult if not impossible.

In August 1939, the Gold Hill Mine was bought by the Northern Cascades Mines, Inc., owned by the Guggenheim family. With its money behind it, the company pressed for a road to the area. But the company also made an agreement with City Light. When Ruby Dam was completed and there still was no road, its equipment would be lifted over the dam by City Light crews and then could be transported to the mines.[5] There also was talk, first about including the area in a national park, followed by the specter of a larger, more restricted wilderness area that might do what everyone feared – stop mining completely.

Ross Dam completed. Seattle Municipal Archives

But it was mostly talk and work continued on the road which was pushed through Hart's Pass and, in rough form, reached the old town of Barron and then the Gold Hill itself. By that time the Guggenheim interests had bought out almost all the Upper Skagit mines, and they had miners scattered around seeking additional properties to develop.

In May 1940, the Forest Service halted all mining and construction work on the Upper Skagit. The order also meant a short delay in construction at Ross Dam, though City Light was allowed to resume work almost immediately. The Forest Service had expanded its plans and wanted to create a large preserve to be called the Glacier Peak Wilderness Area. It would have ended both mining and road building. The Forest Service position wavered through the year and then it changed its mind again and allowed the Guggenheim Co. to resume work. The Forest Service decided to limit its plan to the original, small North Cascade Wilderness Area and it was understood that, if any changes were made, the mines and road would be exempt from all restrictions.[6]

During late 1940 and into 1941, work progressed on the roads, both into the mines from the east and along Ruby Creek. There were plans to reopen the Skagit Queen Mine on Thunder Creek and talk of a road from the Ruby mines to the Thunder Creek mines. What a boom it might have been, had not World War II intervened. The federal government ordered all Skagit mines closed in an effort to provide workers for war production.

The roads became overgrown and the machinery rusted. A few caretakers were left to watch the holdings but the Upper Skagit otherwise was abandoned. When the war ended, the cost of gold and silver was not high enough to reopen the mines. Since then, only the occasional prospector, hiker or weekend camper has wandered through the old mining camps, exploring the deteriorating remains. Someday, perhaps, there will be another boom on the Upper Skagit but the recent creation of a national park in that area makes the prospects rather doubtful.

Chapter 7

RUBY TO THE WAR

The rest of our story focuses more on the technical achievements of dam building than the mystery and intrigue of political maneuvering. At last, we can examine the highlight of Upper Skagit development, the Ruby project or what, after Ross' death, was known as Ross Dam.

Everyone knew from the start that the site known as the Ripraps, just below Ruby Creek, was the best location for a big dam that would create a long lake storing enough water to supply the other installations over the summer and diminish the flood threat that too often hit the lower valley. But building at Ruby was expensive and the project was delayed twice. From 1929 through 1936, City Light quietly bought H.B. Brown's Ruby Creek Inn and any mining claims that might affect construction of the high dam. After the big Skagit flood of 1932, City Light drew plans for a huge dam at Ruby, more than 600 feet high, rising to 1,725 feet above sea level and creating a lake many miles into Canada.[1]

In 1933, City Light applied to the federal government for funds to finish the Diablo Powerhouse and start work at Ruby Creek. But as we have seen, no money was forthcoming.

In 1935, Ross was informed that the Public Works Administration would consider an application to fund construction of the dam at Ruby Creek alone. Though the Diablo plant was unfinished, Ross jumped at the offer. Starting one project before the other was finished was nothing new to him and whenever he saw an opportunity he took it. Ross asked for $13 million for work at Ruby Creek. To show good faith, City Light spent $54,000 seeking a way to extend the railroad to Ruby Creek. That later proved impractical and was abandoned in favor of a plan for a fleet of barges transporting material across Diablo Lake to the site. On Nov. 15, 1936, the PWA granted City Light $3 million to clear timber from Ruby Basin and build a new transmission line to Seattle.[2] It was not exactly what Ross wanted but it was a start. By December, City Light managed to sell more than $4 million worth of bonds, matching the federal grant, and work started on the Ruby project.

Ross was exuberant. "I feel sure," he wrote, "that Ruby Dam will never stop until it is finished."[3] In 1937 there were 50 workers, housed in tents, drilling test holes at the Ruby site and work was well under way on the new transmission line. On Diablo Lake, City Light crews built a floating cookhouse and floating bunkhouses. When they were completed the structures were towed up the lake for the workers. A transmission line was built to carry power from Diablo to Ruby.

It was decided to build the high dam in the form of a variable arch structure which could be completed in three or more separate steps, rather than completing the entire job at one time. The lowest bid received on the first step was nearly $4 million and it

was rejected as too high. City Light tried again few months later and accepted a bid of $5.5 million for a project that included not only the first step of the dam but a bypass tunnel around the site and a work camp. The tunnel was under construction by the end of 1937 and was completed in April 1938. The excavation for the dam was supposed to be completed by the end of 1938 but the exploratory drilling had failed to reveal the extensive work needed and when the year ended the project was well behind schedule. Early in 1939 the workers for the General Shea Company walked off the job and construction stopped until the strike was settled.

Thousands of years ago, when a huge glacier filled the valley above the spot where Ross Dam stands, an ancient waterfall flowed near the ancestor of present day Ruby Creek and it scoured a deep pothole in the river bed. The hole filled with gravel, as did a good deal of the river bed, and when work started on the Ruby Creek Dam, workers found that the bottom of the unsuspected hole was 40 feet below the anticipated level of bedrock. Excavating it delayed work for two months, but the first concrete finally was poured in February 1939 and the new dam started to take shape.[4]

J.D. Ross died In March, while undergoing an operation at the Mayo Clinic, and his assistant, Glenn Smith, was appointed temporary superintendent of Lighting. A few months later, Smith was electrocuted while doing some routine repair work in his home. His body was cremated and the ashes placed in a section of the concrete that was becoming Ross Dam. Eugene R. Hoffman was then named City Light's superintendent.

Work at Ross Dam continued without incident and in January 1940 the first step was complete. The new dam was about 300 feet high. In February, City Light crews began building a 15-foot timber crib dam on top of the concrete structure, raising the level of Ross Lake to a point 1,380 feet above sea level, providing 25 percent more water storage potential than the dam alone provided.

On May 2, 1940, the level of the lake behind the dam reached the top of the crib structure. A few days later, swelled by spring runoff, the water poured over the top, creating a spectacular waterfall. The new Ross Lake was nine miles long and the first step in construction of the dam was complete. How easy it had been compared with the problems faced at Gorge and Diablo. And it would have continued, except for the war.

Chapter 8

The Postwar Boom

The Upper Skagit experienced its most intense building boom from 1943 to 1956. The second and third steps of Ross Dam and Ross Powerhouse were completed, much of the basin behind Ross Dam was cleared, a fourth generator was installed at the Gorge Powerhouse, a new dam was built at Gorge Creek, the Diablo generators were modified and new spillways were added to Diablo Dam. We will examine these projects separately, but they often were overlapping, with several under way simultaneously.

After the first step of Ross Dam was completed, World War II halted construction. Shortly after the war started, however, the federal government urged City Light to complete the Ross Dam second step, pointing out that the added reservoir capacity would increase the generating potential at Diablo and Gorge.[1] But with the war in progress and so much uncertainty, City Light was reluctant to undertake building the 195-foot addition. Nevertheless, the City called for bids, but also applied for a federal grant to help fund the project.[2] When the bids were opened, they estimated the construction costs at about $10 million and because the federal government denied the aid requests, the City rejected the bids.[3]

But the government continued to press City Light and bids were sought again in 1943. This time, a contract was awarded jointly to three companies who agreed to complete the second step for about $9 million. The federal government also gave City Light almost $2 million to help finance the work. The federal money paid for some of the construction that accompanied building the dam itself.[4] To augment the labor supply, the government sent 43 Italian prisoners of war to the Skagit and they worked at Ross and elsewhere.[5]

By March 1945, one crew was busy pouring concrete at the new dam, the wood crib structure atop of the old dam was being removed by others and a third crew was drilling the power tunnel from the dam to the powerhouse. When the war ended the real push started. The contractors immediately hired 300 workers, swelling the workforce and speeding the schedule. Tents were erected on Reflector Bar in Diablo to house the workers and the new settlement was called Hollywood. Over the winter of 1945-46, the weather was unusually bad with heavy snow, work at Ross was stopped briefly and the community of Diablo was isolated by slides that covered the railroad. Five feet of snow fell but after it was cleared progress quickly returned to normal, and it became evident that the second step at Ross would be completed without major problems. City Light decided to go directly to the third step, using the contractors and workforce already there. An additional agreement was negotiated with the General, Shea and Morrison-Knudsen companies, calling for a finished dam 540 feet high.

Concrete generates heat as it hardens and with such a massive block of concrete being laid, it was necessary to find ways to cool it. Tons of dry ice were carted up the valley and in 1948 large refrigeration units were built atop the third step and the liquid they cooled was pumped through more than 100 miles of pipe inside the dam. This was a major accomplishment, considering that every piece of equipment had to be hauled to the site with the awkward barge-ferry system. By the time work on the dam was completed, 20,554 railroad gondola carloads of gravel and 2,558 carloads of cement had been laboriously floated up Diablo Lake.[6]

While the finishing touches were being completed on the dam, there was more snow in February 1948 and a slide crashed into the contractor's camp, destroying many of the houses, killing two workers and starting a fire that burned more of the houses. Slides between Rockport and Diablo hampered attempts of City Light crews to help the stranded victims. Progress was slowed, but it was all completed by the end of the year. Water behind the dam could

then rise to 1,585 feet above sea level and when spillway gates were added to the dam in 1953, the full height of the lake at 1,600 feet was realized.

On August 18, 1949, there was a formal ceremony atop of Ross Dam and City Light officially took possession of its newest creation. The face of the structure was purposely left with hundreds of six-foot-square depressions so that a fourth step could be added at some future date, thickening the dam and raising it to its ultimate height of 1,725 feet above sea level.[7]

Long before the dam was complete, work had started on the powerhouse. Drilling for the foundations started early in 1948 and, in 1949, three generators were ordered from Westinghouse. A rash of postwar labor strikes kept interrupting both the work at Ross and assembly of the generators and schedules were constantly being altered as delay followed delay.[8]

Late in 1949, Peter Kiewit and Sons was awarded the contract to start work on the powerhouse building, along with completion of the penstock tunnels and a few other odds and ends. For some reason, work went badly for the contractor and City Light canceled the contract early in 1951 and ordered the company off the job, claiming that the agreement had been broken. City Light also sued Kiewit for the cost involved in removing its equipment from the Ross site.[9] A month later, the Guy F. Atkinson Co. of Seattle was hired to finish the contract, and after that the job went smoothly. By December 1952, the building was nearly complete and the first generator was in place. At the end of the year, it was running and supplying power to Seattle.[10]

The second generator was online by April 1953 but when the third unit was turned on in May, the scroll case, which carried water into the turbines, ruptured. It took six months to repair the damage but by January 1954, the third Ross unit was running.

In 1952, Superintendent Hoffman proposed adding the fourth step to Ross Dam, in addition to building a high dam at Gorge Creek and a fourth dam farther downstream at Copper Creek.[11] Some preliminary work was begun but Hoffman retired in late 1953 and his replacement, Paul Raver, tabled all of the proposals except for the fourth generator in the Ross Powerhouse. Work started in October 1954 and the machine was in place two years later. All went well until the final tests when, suddenly and unexpectedly, friction in the turbine caused metal parts to expand and before the wheel could be stopped, the turbine seized, stressing on the shaft that connects the turbine with the generator and twisting it slightly. The shaft was only .013 inches out of line but when the generator turned at anything approaching full power, it acted like an out-of-balance automobile wheel and tended to vibrate or rumble.[12] The consultant in charge of the tests quickly evaluated what had happened and then left the scene muttering, "I guess that's about all the damage I can do for today." The problem was corrected about a year later and the generator runs normally today.

When the last generator was in place, Ross Dam and Powerhouse were complete, except for one big headache. Behind the dam, in what was becoming Ross Lake, there was an estimated 340 million board feet of merchantable timber. Unless the timber and the underbrush around it was removed, it would continually rise to the lake surface, float toward the dam and block the power tunnel intakes or just become a nuisance. And the worst problem was that Diablo Dam and Ross Dam effectively blocked access into the basin from the lower valley. No company bid on or offered to remove the timber.

In 1942, City Light had negotiated tentative agreements with the Canadian government allowing Ross Lake to back up eight miles into British Columbia when the dam reached its full height. City Light agreed to buy or rent whatever land was flooded. With that agreement, along with assurances that access into the basin would be possible through

Canada, the Morris, McEkkar and Decco Construction Co. took a contract to begin the clearing. City Light built a floating camp which could be moved around the lake. In 1946, the Walton Lumber Co. of Everett and a Canadian firm agreed to remove timber from the area, transport it north into Canada, float it down the Fraser River into Puget Sound and then to Everett. The cut logs were loaded on special trucks, 60 feet long and 16 feet wide, which were transported to the area in pieces and reassembled.[13]

At the north end of what was becoming Ross Lake, at a place called Hozomeen near the Canadian border, a camp was built, and a third company began removing brush and timber from the areas that would be flooded, both on the American and Canadian sides of the border. It became obvious that all of the timber would never be harvested, but the crews worked as fast as they could in the time allowed.

In addition to cutting the timber, the Forest Service insisted that City Light rebuild at higher levels any trails that would be flooded. That work was complete in 1953 and on March 26, 1953, Ross Lake touched Canadian soil for the first time. City Light then paid the British Columbia government $250,000 for the right to flood 5,475 acres. In 1954, City Light and the Canadian government tried to reach agreement allowing long-term flooding of the Canadian land, through an international joint commission meeting in Washington, D.C., but no permanent pact was reached. City Light did obtain an understanding that the situation would be re-negotiated yearly, that the lake would rise no higher than 1,600 feet and that a $5,000 fee would be paid each year.[14]

Efforts to cut the remaining timber were abandoned in 1958. There were experiments to determine if divers could be sent down into the cold water to fell the trees, allowing them to float to the surface. One man died testing the unworkable plan. The Ross Lake surface was covered with debris and City Light crews at both the floating camp and Hozomeen labored to clear and burn the flotsam. That job continued for some years after 1959. Except for cleaning the lake and a few other loose ends, however, work at Ross was at an end.

City Light had considered upgrading the old wooden dam at Gorge Creek even before 1947. With the postwar boom under way, ample funds and little political trouble, renovation plans took shape. City Light decided to build a new structure about seven feet higher than the old one with steel flashboards and some spillgates. And it would be made of concrete.[15] By late 1948, the Cascade Construction Co. and the Alton Phillips Co. had started work at what Upper Skagit residents called "The East End," building the second dam at Gorge Creek.

The winter of 1948-49 was one of the worst on record in the Upper Valley. From early December there was heavy snow, slides, flooding and ice. Slides cut power and pushed transmission poles into the river, along with parts of the railroad and trees. The debris in the river slammed into the old dam, ripping parts of it away, and leveling the flashboards. The slides isolated the construction site and finally it was necessary to close the Gorge Powerhouse, drain the power tunnel and use it as a route through which stranded workers could be evacuated.

If that was not enough, there was a heavy rain – five inches – followed by more slides and flooding. The Gorge intake was jammed with debris and the powerhouse was useless. The power tunnel was again drained, workers were evacuated and equipment and food was packed through it and on upriver to the stranded community at Diablo.[16] The bad weather maintained its momentum until late February and life began returning to normal. It was mid-March before routine travel between Newhalem and Diablo was re-established.

Despite the problems, crews were busy pouring concrete for the new dam by midsummer and the work continued uneventfully through the summer of 1949. The heavy rains and snow began again the following December. The river flooded, taking out two bridges between Newhalem and Rockport. The Gorge intake was plugged with debris and the Skagit Flats downstream were under water. As if adding insult to injury, the temperature dropped to six below zero, with more heavy snow.[17] At that point, the contractor moved his crews out for the rest of the winter.

Work crews returned to Gorge Creek late in February and by April 1950 the dam was finished. A year later, the final touches were completed and the contractor removed all its equipment and buildings. Late in 1951, City Light crews removed the original wood weir behind the new dam. To everyone's surprise, the old dam was quite sound and in excellent condition. In fact, it was so sturdy that parts of it had to be blasted away.[18]

City Light had always assumed that the new dam was only a temporary structure, that one day a high dam would be built at Gorge Creek. In the meantime, the water storage capacity had been increased and the reservoir elevation raised almost 10 feet. More power could be produced in the Gorge Powerhouse.

There were plans back in the 1920s to someday increase the size of the Gorge Powerhouse. It was believed the building size would be doubled and three more generators, similar to the original three, would be added. But the years had brought improved technology and generators far larger than the originals could be built. City Light itself had pioneered some of the advances with the generators at Diablo. With this in mind, the Gorge tunnel was investigated in 1944 to determine how much water it could supply to the existing and additional equipment. The tunnel was found to be basically sound and would easily supply a fourth generator which could be substantially larger than the units already there. It was decided to add the new generator at the north end of the powerhouse. A new power tunnel would branch off the old one and carry water to the new generator. There would also be a new transmission line from Gorge to Seattle.[19]

All the construction upstream necessitated a few postponements but work started on the powerhouse addition in July 1948 and by year's end, work was well under way. A generator more than double the size of the original three was ordered from Westinghouse. The hard winter of 1948-49 slowed progress at Gorge Powerhouse, as it did upstream. But by May 1949 crews were connecting the new power tunnel addition, removing the relief valves from the central adit, adding a concrete plug in its place and enlarging the surge tank that rose above the power tunnel near the powerhouse. The three original generators were remodeled, the operator's room was renovated and, in the midst of all that progress, it still was necessary to use mules to install the high line that stretched across the valley and allowed equipment and concrete to be lifted and over the river to the construction site.[20] In October the old generators were back in service. By mid-1951, the new generator was undergoing tests while additions were being made to the electrical switching yard that sat across the river. The Gorge Powerhouse was complete.

The remodeling at Gorge seemed such a good idea that City Light decided to improve Diablo as well. In 1950, additions were made to the spillways, allowing the water to fall into the canyon without eroding the natural rock walls. In 1952, 36 houses were built for the families of those who worked at Diablo, bringing the total number of houses there to 55. A smaller version of the incline hoist, big enough to hold five or six men and called a "man lift," was built next to the old incline that had handled railroad cars during Diablo and Ross construction. The contractor's camp on Diablo Lake, a mile above the dam, which

had been used during Ross Dam construction, was offered for sale to anyone who would use it as a resort. There was a buyer, and a successful business began in that area.

Since the 1920s, the Forest Service was gradually changing its attitudes toward conservation. With that came a realization that the Skagit dams had done more harm to fish runs than had been originally estimated. In 1946, the Department of Fisheries demanded that City Light maintain a minimum flow in the Skagit River, keeping enough water below Gorge Dam at all times to guarantee no further damage to the fish habitat. Stiff fines were to be paid if the flow of water dropped below the minimum. And in 1947, after long negotiations, City Light agreed to contribute more than $50,000 to the construction of a state fish hatchery at Marblemount and to maintain those ponds for nine years. A clear attempt was being made to re-establish the salmon runs and the effort paid off when, after a few years, the migrating fish again began to appear in the river, only below Gorge Dam, however.[21]

To educate the children of Newhalem and Diablo residents, City Light agreed in 1949 to pay $160,000 toward building a high school in Concrete. In 1951, an annual payment by City Light to help with school operation was approved. City Light bought buses to transport students from Diablo and Newhalem, which meant they traveled 80 miles round trip to school every day. Grade schools were built in both Newhalem and Diablo so only high school students were bused.

New houses were built for workers in Newhalem. Long-distance telephone service reached the camp in 1948. In 1951 the community was threatened by a forest fire that raced down Goodell Creek. Plans were made for a hasty evacuation but, as happened once before, a wind diverted the flames and the town remained untouched. Dana Currier, the first Skagit supervisor, retired in 1954 and in 1958, when the old meeting hall – or barn as some called it – was replaced with a new auditorium, it was named Currier Hall.

In 1939, shortly after the death of J.D. Ross, the road to Newhalem had been opened and in the 1940s and 1950s many of the bridges between Rockport and Diablo were rebuilt. In 1954, a microwave communications network was installed that allowed the various parts of the project to contact each other, no matter how bad the weather. The Upper Skagit was no longer isolated and was enjoying more amenities than it had ever known before.

From 1948 through 1954, City Light spent more than $55 million building the Skagit. It was a sizable investment and it created one of the more important hydroelectric developments in the Pacific Northwest. There were only two projects left on the drawing boards; the addition to the top of Ross Dam and construction of the final Gorge High Dam.

Skagit headwaters. Whatcom Museum of History & Art

Chapter 9

Back Where We Started

We have come full circle and return now to Gorge Creek, where City Light started building in 1917 and where, ironically enough, it would build its last Skagit dam. In 1949, when Ross Dam had been completed and work on its powerhouse was beginning, City Light was heady with its postwar success and began investigating a new location for a dam. It settled on Copper Creek, downstream from Newhalem,[1] but the state Game Commission determined that such a dam would destroy one of the finest remaining fish-producing streams in the Puget Sound area.[2]

But in 1953, City Light was back at Copper Creek and requested preliminary permits to develop the site. Exploratory drilling went on through 1956 with minor work stretching on into 1958. City Light abandoned Copper Creek in 1959, with the understanding that consideration of the site could be reopened if City Light wished. Interest in Copper Creek declined because City Light had decided to build the High Gorge Dam, had acquired a power site location in Eastern Washington, had failed to find adequate footings for a dam and had not been able to resolve environmental issues, especially where the fish were concerned.

It was Gorge Dam or nothing. The permits for Gorge construction were obtained in 1951, the surveys and preliminary drilling were conducted through 1952 and into late 1953. A dam 300 feet high would be built. Since it would flood the railroad track between Gorge Creek and Diablo, and since relocation of the railroad at a higher elevation would involve grades steeper than any conventional engine could negotiate, it was decided to remove the tracks and replace them with a road.[3] Upper Skagit residents, understandably nostalgic about the railroad, were upset. They quickly forgot the inconveniences that the railroad frequently caused and remembered the romance of the old Baldwin steam engine, and the quaint electric cars that hauled them up and down the valley. But the railroad had to go and a crew started removing the track in mid-1954. Everything went except the incline lift that was still necessary to transport heavy loads up to the level of Diablo Dam and on to Ross and the steam engine that was kept as a reminder of an era that was ending. By the end of the year, the remains of the railroad were gone and it was officially out of service early in 1955. As Mayor Brown of Seattle had said years before, it had never been as long as many other railroads, but it was every bit as wide.

Work proceeded on the new road that would connect Newhalem with Diablo. That road, which ultimately would become a link in the North Cascades Highway, was carved into the hillside at a high elevation, taking it well above the level of the anticipated Gorge reservoir. Three tunnels were necessary, in addition to a costly bridge spanning Gorge Creek. It was completed in 1957 and the state Highway Department announced plans to extend it an additional seven miles to Thunder Creek where there would be a public campground giving access to Diablo Lake.[4] That road was nearly complete in 1960. In 1962, the Newhalem-to-Thunder Creek road was widened to two lanes.

At Gorge Creek, the plans envisioned a combination gravity-arch dam. Part of the dam would be nothing more than a huge block of concrete held in place by the force of gravity. The other part would be built in the shape of a slender arch using that principle to absorb the force of the water behind the dam. It required less concrete than a gravity type. The topography ruled out an entire arch type, as were Ross and Diablo dams. Two companies, Merritt, Chapman and Scott of New York and Savin Construction of Connecticut, made the low bid of nearly $15 million as a joint venture. That delighted City Light engineers who had estimated the cost at nearer $17 million.[5] The job was to take four years.

The first task was digging down to bedrock. It had long been known that the riverbed was deep with gravel and that a good deal of the river flow was through the gravel rather than over it.

Though there might be a temporary dam to divert the river from the excavation, as soon as a hole was dug it would fill with water from the subsurface flow. But City Light had planned to solve the problem with a complicated ice curtain. A series of pipes would be sunk into the gravel just upstream from the excavation and a saltwater solution, cooled to well below freezing, then would be pumped through the pipes. Engineers hoped the water in the gravel around the pipes would freeze, eventually making a wall of ice more than 200 feet deep, 260 feet long and four inches thick. In case any water seeped through the curtain, seven pump wells would keep the excavation dry.[6]

City Light built the ice curtain and the contractor started digging. But by early February 1957 it was clear something was wrong. There was water in the hole and not just a little bit. The contractor had to stop work while City Light crews investigated and discovered the ice curtain was hardly deep enough. In fact, it missed its required depth by more than 100 feet.

At that point, the contractors claimed that City Light had not fulfilled its part of the contract and demanded that the agreement be renegotiated or terminated. City Light countered that the contractors were being unrealistic and had failed to comply fully with the instructions detailed in their contract.[7]

Nothing happened at Gorge Creek until early 1958 and in the meantime the excavation turned into a large lake. City Light agreed to negotiate with the contractor and, at the same time, installed large pumps to push more saltwater through the network of pipes, succeeding in stopping the flow of water into the excavation. By then work at Gorge was more than a year behind schedule. The water was pumped out of the excavation and work started again. When the gravel was removed, it was discovered that the riverbed at the dam site was shaped something like a W if viewed in a cross-section diagram. More digging than anticipated was required and the excavation became quite deep with the pit on the south side of the W being deeper than on the north side. Finally, almost two years behind schedule, Superintendent Paul Raver and Seattle Mayor Clinton were lowered into the hole to pour the first concrete. What a glorious time the Seattle newspapers of the 1920s and 1930s would have had with the problems, but in the 1950s it was all back-page news.

The weather was not cooperative that winter and a rock and earth slide tumbled into the excavation, covering sections of the concrete and damaging some of the pumps that maintained the

curtain of ice.[8] Then there was heavy snow, Diablo was isolated and the road to Gorge Creek was blocked by slides. It was 1959 and City Light applied to the government to extend the construction permits on the Gorge site. When the snow melted, work continued on a round-the-clock basis through the rest of that year. By March 1960 the dam was two-thirds complete.[9]

At the Gorge Powerhouse, the four generators were rebuilt to operate with the higher head of water that would be formed behind the new dam. Off and on, it was necessary to close down the powerhouse so that the Gorge intake could be modified and other improvements made. By the end of 1960, the spillway gates were in place, water was accumulating on the lake and the old road and dam were submerged for the first time. At a formal ceremony January 6, 1961, the mayor and superintendent of Lighting took possession of the new dam. The honors, appropriately enough, had to be held inside a small building near the dam because of bad weather. There was one other sour note. The dam had cost more than $29 million, about twice the contractor's estimate.[10] City Light and the contractor fought about the matter in court until 1965, with City Light finally paying the contractor for a large percentage of the additional costs. The work at Gorge Creek was done.[11]

There is a footnote to the story. Some years after the completion of the Gorge Creek High Dam, the small Newhalem Creek Powerhouse, City Light's first Skagit generator, overheated and burned to the ground. After some consideration, both of its practical and historical value, City Light rebuilt the unit, rehabilitated the generator and it remains in operation today.

So we really did come full circle. By the time Gorge High Dam was complete, City Light was well into construction of its $125 million Boundary Dam on the Pend Oreille River in Pend Oreille County. For the time being, the Skagit hydroelectric development, which altogether had cost more than $250 million, was finished.

Epilogue

Completion of the high dam at Gorge Creek hardly ends the Upper Skagit story. Since January 1961, much has happened in the valley. Work continued on the North-Cross-State Highway, Washington Route 20. On Sept. 29, 1968, Gov. Dan Evans and U.S. Sen. Warren Magnuson led a group of officials who used Jeeps to make the first official trip over the new road. The route took them past Ross Lake, Whistler Mountain and through Rainy and Washington passes into the Methow Valley.[1] There still was considerable work left on the road, but it finally opened to the general public late in the summer of 1972 and was in full use in 1973. The story of its construction and the controversy over its route will make another chapter in the Upper Skagit story, if not a complete book. The growing influence of environmentalists, which we have seen emerging over the years, was apparent while the highway was being built.

On Oct. 2, 1968, the North Cascades National Park was created. Again, the long debate that surrounded that action will not be covered here but, needless to say, environmentalists were active in those discussions too. The park is divided into two sections, north and south of the Skagit hydroelectric development. The area around the river not included in the park was named the Ross Lake National Recreation Area and administration shifted from the Forest Service to the National Park Service.[2]

U.S. Sen. Warren Magnuson and Gov. Dan Evans lead a group of officials opening the North Cascades Highway in 1968. Whatcom Museum of History & Art

In July 1972, City Light started automating the Gorge Powerhouse. When that was completed, the two other powerhouses also were automated. This allows City Light to operate the powerhouses with only a small crew and support personnel.

Over its first 100 years, from the 1870s through the 1970s, the Upper Skagit was transformed from a frontier wilderness to a developed national park. The federal government first allowed the area to be exploited by anyone in any way. Then controls emerged and the federal government ruled that the natural riches of the Cascades would be developed by those who could benefit the largest number of citizens, primarily through large and well-financed companies. On the Skagit, it was further decided that a publicly owned developer would preferable over private enterprise. Since then, the public has become more conscious of environmental concerns that were not understood a century ago. It is the same chain of events which has determined the use and development of much of U.S. public lands. The story of the Upper Skagit reduces this process of historical evolution to a scale where it can be studied and understood and the Upper Skagit will continue to serve that role for many years into the future.

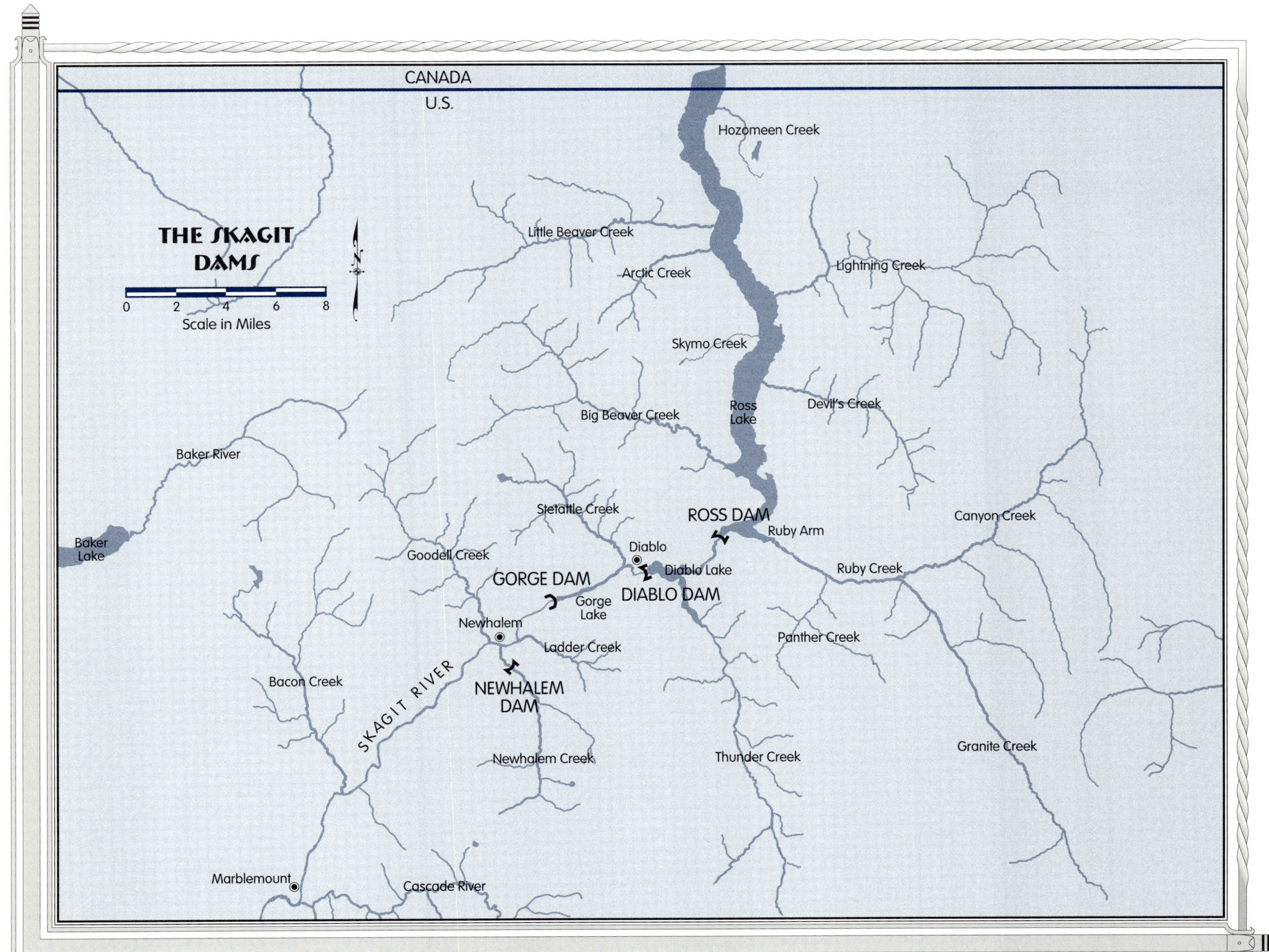
THE SKAGIT DAMS
CANADA
U.S.
0
2
4
6
8
Scale in Miles
N
Hozomeen Creek
Little Beaver Creek
Arctic Creek
Lightning Creek
Skymo Creek
Ross Lake
Devil's Creek
Big Beaver Creek
Baker River
Baker Lake
Stetattle Creek
ROSS DAM
Ruby Arm
Canyon Creek
Diablo
Goodell Creek
Diablo Lake
Ruby Creek
GORGE DAM
DIABLO DAM
Gorge Lake
Newhalem
Ladder Creek
Panther Creek
Bacon Creek
SKAGIT RIVER
NEWHALEM DAM
Newhalem Creek
Thunder Creek
Granite Creek
Marblemount
Cascade River

Skagit River Hydroelectric Development Chronology

I. Gorge Creek Dam and Powerhouse

Started:	*1918*	
Dam finished:	*1924*	*(wood crib dam)*
First Generator:	*1924*	*30,000 kw*
Second Generator:	*1925*	*30,000 kw*
Third Generator:	*1929*	*33,000 kw*
Fourth Generator:	*1951*	*66,700 kw*

Second dam finished: 1950 (concrete diversion type)
Third (High) dam finished: 1961 (gravity-arch type 300 feet high)

II. Diablo Dam and Powerhouse

Dam started:	*1927*		
Dam finished:	*1929*	*(modified arch type)*	*389 feet*
First Generator:	*1936*	*78,000 kw*	
Second Generator:	*1937*	*78,000 kw*	

Two house units of 1,500 kw each

III. Ross Dam and Powerhouse (Ruby Project)

Dam started:	*1937*	
First step complete:	*1940-300 feet high*	
Second step complete:	*1946-195 feet high*	
Third step complete:	*1949-45 feet high (540 foot total)*	
	(Dam is variable arch type)	
First Generator:	*1952*	*90,000 kw*
Second Generator:	*1953*	*90,000 kw*
Third Generator:	*1954*	*90,000 kw*
Fourth Generator:	*1956*	*90,000 kw*

IV. Newhalem Power Plant

Project started: *1919*
Project first in operation: 1921
Generator: *1921* *2,000 kw*

FOOTNOTES

GENERAL WORKS

1. Pitzer, Paul C., "A History of the Upper Skagit Valley. 1880-1924," Unpublished Master's Thesis, University of Washington, 1966
2. Pitzer, Paul C., "A History of the Upper Skagit Valley, 1924-1961," Unpublished manuscript, 1972.

CHAPTER I

1. Ethel van Fleet Harris, "Early Historical Incidents of Skagit County," an unpublished manuscript in the Northwest Collection, University of Washington, 1932, p. 25. And Violet Burmaster, "The History of Skagit County," an unpublished manuscript in the Northwest Collection, University of Washington, 1931, p. 5.
2. U.S. Forest Service, "The Mount Baker Almanac," pp. 17 and 63. And Bellingham Bay Mail, Bellingham, Wash., March 15, 1879 (microfilm from Bancroft Library, Berkeley, Calif.).
3. Ibid.
4. Bellingham Bay Mail, April 19, 1879.
5. Ibid. Dec. 20, 1879.
6. Ibid. May 1, 1880.
7. Unidentified newspaper clipping, Glee Davis scrapbook, private collection, Sedro Woolley, Wash.
8. Concrete Herald, May 21, 1935.
9. U.S. Forest Service, "The Mount Baker Almanac," pp. 193-194.
10. Concrete Herald, March 21, 1935.
11. Mount Vernon Argus, "Illustrated Annual," April 17, 1908.
12. "Clean Money," published brochure in the file for The Skagit Queen Mines, Mount Baker National Forest Files, Federal Records Center, Seattle, Wash. (this collection will be called the Mount Baker MSS).

CHAPTER II

1. Statutes at Large. Vol. XXIV, Pt. 2, pp. 233-234. June 11, 1906, Government Printing Office, 1907.
2. Administrative Site Withdrawal, "Report," Reflector Bar File, May 29, 1908, Mount Baker MSS, box 23219.

3. August Dohne claim "Report," Dec. 8, 1908, August Dohne file, Mount Baker MSS, box 28220, and interview with Glee Davis, Nov. 14, 1964.
4. Ibid.
5. Ibid. and, Conrad to Park, November 28, 1908, August Dohne file, Mount Baker MSS.
6. Park to Conrad, Dec. 7, 1908, August Dohne file, Mount Baker MSS.
7. Conrad to Park, Jan. 2, 1909, August Dohne File, Mount Baker MSS.
8. Park to Portland Office, March 8, 1909, August Dohne File, Mount Baker MSS.
9. Homestead Application, Burton Babcock File, Mount Baker MSS, and Glee Davis interview. Mr. Davis knew Burton Babcock and saw the Garland letters to Babcock. Those letters are now lost.
10. Garland to Pinchot, Sept. 24, 1908, Burton Babcock File, Mount Baker MSS.
11. Garland to Pinchot, Oct. 1, 1908, Burton Babcock File, Mount Baker MSS.

CHAPTER III

1. Cedar Bar Register, July 1904. This log of visitors to the Upper Skagit is held by Glee Davis, Sedro Woolley, Wash.
2. Parker, "Skagit Project Feasibility," Exhibit 20. From papers held by the Puget Sound Power and Light Co., Bellevue, Wash. And, undated and unidentified clipping; Anacortes American, Jan. 30, 1913, found among papers from the Seattle City Light and James Delmage Ross collection, held by the University of Washington. called the J.D. Ross MSS.
3. Seattle Times, Dec. 25, 1917, and Concrete Herald, Dec, 29, 1917.
4. Ross to Hanson, April 25, 1918, J.D. Ross MSS.
5. Cecil to Hanson. May 21, 1918, Mount Baker MSS.
6. Landes to Dimock. Aug. 22, 1918. J.D. Ross MSS.
7. Concrete Herald, Feb. 1, 1919. And, unidentified clippings, Jan. 29, 1919, found in scrapbooks held by Jim Ross (nephew of J.D. Ross) of Seattle Wash., called Ross Scrapbooks.
8. Concrete Herald, Sept. 20, 1919.
9. Concrete Herald, Jan. 24, 1920, and Sattle Times, Jan. 17, 1919, Ross Scrapbooks.
10. Concrete Herald, April 3, and May 8, 1920. And Forest Service memorandum, March 8, 1920. Mount Baker MSS.
11. Cecil to Washington D.C., March 31, 1920. Mount Baker MSS and Dater to Uhden, March 27, 1920, Mount Baker MSS.
12. Concrete Herald. April 16, 1921.
13. Seattle Star, Feb. 11, 1924.
14. Seattle Star, Feb. 6-15, 1924.
15. Seattle Union Record, July 31, 1924.
16. Ross memorandum. Feb. 27, 1924, J.D. Ross MSS.

CHAPTER IV

1. Seattle Star, Jan. 27, 1926, and Seattle Times, Jan. 27, 1926.
2. Gorge Powerhouse Log, Oct. 17. 1924. The senior operator at each powerhouse is responsible for keeping a log or journal in which he makes entries at the end of each shift. These logs are on file at each powerhouse.
3. Seattle Post Intelligencer, Jan. 8, 1925.
4. Seattle Star, Oct.16, 1925.
5. City Light Annual Report, 1925, p. 33 and Ross to Brown, Oct. 31, 1925, J.D. Ross MSS.
6. Ross to City Council, June 6, 1927, J.D. Ross MSS.
7. Seattle Post Intelligencer, Sept. 10, 1927.
8. City Council bills, Nov. 8. 1927, J.D. Ross MSS, and Seattle Post Intelligencer, Nov. 10, 1927.
9. Glen Smith to City Council, February 18, 1928, J.D. Ross MSS.
10. Seattle Post Intelligencer, June 6. 1929.
11. Ibid. November 2, 1928.
12. Ross to City Council, Oct. 1, 1929, JOD. Ross MSS.
13. Gorge Powerhouse Log, Oct. 4. 1929.
14. Seattle Post Intelligencer, Aug. 27, 1930.
15. "J.D. Ross, Public Power Magnate," Harper's Magazine, June 1940, p. 53.
16. Ibid., p. 53.
17. Skagit Valley Herald. March 31, 1932, and Concrete Herald, March 31, 1932.
18. Seattle City Light Annual Report, 1933, p. 55 and 56.
19. Seattle Star, July 11, 1933.
20. "Diablo Generator Construction Report," Sept., 1926, J.D. Ross MSS.

CHAPTER V

1. Seattle Times, July 26, 1924.
2. Ross to Umlauff, Sept. 20, 1929, J.D. Ross MSS.
3. Ross to R.F.C., Aug. 12, 1932, J.D. Ross MSS.
4. Press Release, July 10, 1935, J.D. Ross MSS.
5. Ross to Kane, Aug. 22, 1934, Ross MSS.

1. Azurite Mining Co. to Ross, Jan. 6, 1934, J.D. Ross MSS.
2. Concrete Herald, July 2, 1936.
3. Buck to Forester, Feb. 8, 1928, and Holland to Kellingham, Dec. 6, 1937, Ruby Road Project File, Mount Baker MSS.
4. City Light News, Sept. 1939.
5. Thompson to Flory, March 25, 1940, Mount Baker MSS.
6. Granger to Wilderness Society, May 15, 1940, Mount Baker, MSS.

CHAPTER VII

1. Ruby Dam plans, March 23, 1933, J.D. Ross MSS.
2. Glen Smith Press Release, Dec. 28, 1936, J.D. Ross MSS.
3. Ross to Jorgensen, Jan. 16, 1937, J.D. Ross MSS.
4. Concrete Herald, Feb. 23, 1939.

CHAPTER VIII

1. Concrete Herald, Jan. 29, 1942.
2. Ibid., Sept. 17,1942.
3. Ibid., Jan. 28, 1943 and Feb. 18, 1943, and Engineering News Record, Sept. 20, 1945. Vol. 135, p. 378.
4. Annual Report, 1943, p. 9.
5. Seattle City Light News, Oct., 1943.
6. Skagit Static, Nov. 22, 1947, Feb. 14, 1948, and Seattle City Light News, Feb. 1948. (Skagit Static was a local newsletter published by some of the residents of Newhalem.)
7. Seattle City Light News, Sept. 1949, and Seattle City Light Annual Report, 1950, p. 10.
8. Westinghouse to City Light, Nov. 2, 1949, From papers held by Seattle City Light, hereafter called the Seattle City Light MSS.
9. Concrete Herald, Feb. 22, 1951.
10. Ross Powerhouse Log, Dec. 22 through 31, 1952, and interviews with Jack Roper, Ross Powerhouse supervisor.
11. Concrete Herald, May 28, 1952.
12. Ross Powerhouse Logs, 1954 through 1957.
13. Hoffman to Public Works, Dec. 21, 1951, City Light MSS, and "The Skagit Story" by Carl L. Cooper, 1956, a Post Intelligencer publication, p. 15.
14. Newsletter, April 22, 1954, Seattle City Light MSS.
15. Skagit Static, July 19, 1947.
16. Gorge Powerhouse Log, Feb. 26, 1949.
17. Skagit Static, Jan. 14, 1950.
18. Gorge Powerhouse Log, Aug. 11, 1951.
19. Skagit Static, Nov. 29, 1947.
20. Skagit Static, Oct. 8. 1949.
21. Concrete Herald, 1950.

CHAPTER IX

1. Fisheries to Hoffman, Oct. 17, 1945, City Light MSS., and Concrete Herald, July 31, 1947.
2. Permit Application, Oct. 23, 1953, City Light MSS.
3. Permits, Jan. 1951, City Light MSS.
4. Concrete Herald, Jan. 1946, and Skagit Static, Aug. 1946.
5. Seattle City Light News, April, 1957, and Concrete Herald, Sept. 12, 1957, and April 21, 1960.
6. Concrete Herald, Dec. 2, 1954.
7. Concrete Herald, Feb. 16, 1965, and "Newsletter," March 15. 1956, City Light MSS.
8. Concrete Herald, Feb. 14, 1957.
9. Concrete Herald, Nov. 13, 1958.
10. Concrete Herald, June 9, 1950.
11. Newsletter, Jan. 12, 1961, City Light MSS.

EPILOGUE

1. Seattle Times, Sept. 30, 1968.
2. Seattle Times, Oct. 6, 1968.